ELIZABETH AND IVY

ROBERT LIDDELL

ELIZABETH
AND IVY

◇ ◇ ◇

With an Introduction by
FRANCIS KING

PETER OWEN
London and Chicago

PETER OWEN PUBLISHERS
20 Holland Park Avenue, London W11 3QU
www.peterowen.com

Peter Owen books are distributed in the USA and Canada by
Independent Publishers Group/Trafalgar Square
814 North Franklin Street, Chicago, IL 60610, USA

First published in Great Britain by Peter Owen Publishers 1986
© Robert Liddell 1986
Introduction © Francis King 1986

ISBN 978-0-7206-0644-7

A catalogue record for this book is available from the British Library.

To

Joanna Kingham
in loving memory of Elizabeth

CONTENTS

INTRODUCTION

Robert Liddell describes this book as an attempt 'to give some account of my friendship with two distinguished writers'. What modesty prevents him from even implying in the course of his narrative is that he himself is a writer of great distinction. This distinction embraces a far wider spectrum of literature than that of his two friends. As a critic, he has produced excellent studies of Jane Austen and George Eliot and two books on the novel, *A Treatise on the Novel* and *Some Principles of Fiction*, that have taken their place alongside Henry James's *The Art of the Novel*, E.M. Forster's *Aspects of the Novel* and Percy Lubbock's *The Craft of Fiction*. As a travel writer, he has made himself indispensable to scholarly, discriminating travellers with such works as *Aegean Greece* and *Byzantium and Istanbul*. As a biographer, he is author of a pioneering life of the Alexandrian Greek poet Cavafy. His novels include *Unreal City*, in which Cavafy appears as a leading character; *The Last Enchantments*, about which Elizabeth Taylor and I independently wrote him fan-letters; and *Stepsons*, a fictionalized account of his appalling childhood and adolescence after the death of his beloved mother. Why then is he not better known to the public at large?

The chief reason must surely be that, since 1947, he has never chosen to visit this country. Except in the case of a writer as famous as Graham Greene, Somerset Maugham or Muriel Spark, out of sight is too often out of mind, where readers and reviewers are concerned. Another reason, I should guess, is that the virtues of balance, reticence and decorum, so evident in this work as in everything else that he has written, may strike the hurried and unheeding as old-fashioned. No doubt it was on those grounds that his publishers of many years, Jonathan Cape, abruptly severed their connection with him, at the same time that they took the identical step with his friend Barbara Pym. Fortunately, unlike her, Robert Liddell was soon able to find another, more appreciative publisher.

Robert Liddell's often given reason for not visiting England after the death of his only brother in the last war is that thenceforward 'my life was broken there'. For many years there was also the lowering presence of his long-lived stepmother, so vividly described in *Stepsons*. With her he wished at all costs to avoid a confrontation that could only be, at best, acutely embarrassing, and, at worst, a painful revival of childhood memories. After her death, many of his friends urged him at last to return. But by then it was too late. Clearly, he was in the same position as someone who has taken so long a leave of absence from a job that he feels that he cannot return to it, though begged to do so – those of the staff who have not left will have changed their posts, the office routine will no longer be comprehensible, he will arrive as a stranger among strangers.

As Mr Liddell reveals, he never saw Ivy Compton-Burnett after 1947 and less than a dozen times before that date; and his encounters with Elizabeth Taylor were also few and brief. Yet between him and each of them there developed a friendship far closer than between many people who see each other daily. Ivy Compton-Burnett always spoke of him to me as of some nephew much loved and never forgotten, though for so many years sadly 'lost to foreign parts' (the phrase was hers). 'One would think that he would wish to come home,' she remarked on more than one occasion, not realizing that for him home was now more likely to be his flat on the Lycabettus, with its magnificent panorama of Athens, than a room in an hotel or in the house or flat of some friend in England. Whenever I came back from Greece, she would at once ask me for news of him – guessing rightly that, such was his habitual discretion, there was much that she was obliged to read between the lines in his letters and some things that she could not read there at all.

Her deep regard for him, demonstrated by her act of making him one of her six residuary legatees, was, as I see it, founded on two rocks. The first was gratitude for his study *The Novels of Ivy Compton-Burnett* (1955), published at a time when her fame was more circumscribed than it is today. All novelists wish their work to be liked; but, especially if they are good novelists, they all also wish their work to be understood. It was Robert's understanding, which she frequently contrasted with what she saw as Pamela Hansford Johnson's obtuseness in a British Council pamphlet, that made her feel particularly in his debt. The second rock was her sympathy for someone who, like herself, had suffered an oppressive childhood and adolescence and had lost a beloved brother in a war. Of Robert's novel *Stepsons* she remarked to me: 'He has done nothing finer.' Then she added after a pause: 'But one must confess that from time to time one could not help feeling a pang of sympathy for that awful woman.' Unlike Robert, Ivy had not merely suffered under a family tyrant but had been one herself, and she knew that the second of these two roles is often as unenviable as the first.

Robert Liddell reports, at second hand, that Ivy remarked of Elizabeth: 'She is a young woman who looks as if she never had to wash her gloves.' If indeed she said this, it must have been early in their friendship – which began not, as Hilary Spurling, Ivy's biographer, suggests, as the result of an introduction from Robert but after the younger woman had written the older one a fan-letter. Like many people insecure about their own social origins, Ivy was always curious about the social origins of others, so that 'Somehow I cannot quite place him (or her)' was a comment one often heard her make. Learning that one of my sisters had known Elizabeth in her early years, she asked me to ask her if it were true that Elizabeth had once been a governess. When I relayed the answer as Yes, Ivy tucked in her chin, looked down into her bosom, gave a small smile and said, 'One had thought so.'

Reading the extracts from Elizabeth's letters published here, I felt first exhilaration and then sadness: exhilaration because I had the illusion that I was once again in the presence of the witty, humane and humorous woman whom I once knew; sadness because death snatched her away so prematurely, when she was at the height of her creative powers. Ivy took the same admiring pleasure in Elizabeth's elegance and femininity as she did in that of Madge Ashton (Garland), wife of Sir Leigh Ashton, director of the Victoria and Albert Museum, and an authority on fashion. Ivy's and Elizabeth's qualities were, in most respects, complementary;

yet they had in common a quality that I can best describe as 'trueness'.

Friendships have a life-cycle, and sometimes this life-cycle is shorter than those of the people who are partners in them. Some time before the close of Ivy's long life, I sensed that the life-cycle of the friendship between her and Elizabeth was nearing its end. There was no row, no rancour, nothing but affection and respect; but Elizabeth seemed to appear less and less at Ivy's tea-table and in her conversation. Perhaps the two women, each possessed of formidable powers of intuition, now knew all there was to know about each other, and any contact between them had staled because it lacked the previous excitement of mutual discovery. That Elizabeth was not among Ivy's literary friends at her funeral in Putney Vale Crematorium probably has no significance; she may well have been ill, abroad or fulfilling some other unavoidable engagement. But, unlike Robert Liddell, I think there is significance in the omission of her from a will in which Ivy was otherwise so scrupulous about remembering all her nearest friends.

That Elizabeth did not make a seventh to the company of six writers who were each bequeathed a looking-glass, Mr Liddell sees as wholly natural – the omission 'may have been a tribute to her good taste; she would have had no room in her house for such an object. Perhaps it was also a tribute to her good looks (if Ivy were really being naughty): Elizabeth need not have feared to face it'. But, however crowded the house, who would not have cherished such a memento of so great a writer? And if Ivy had not wished to leave Elizabeth a looking-glass, with possibly mischievous implications, why did she not, as in the case of Madge Ashton, James Lees-Milne, Cecil Gould and others, leave her something else?

Inevitably, when people write letters to friends, they attempt to present only the best of themselves; and if those people are writers, that attempt is usually successful. It was therefore the best of these two remarkable women that Robert Liddell generally apprehended and now here transmits. But their best was also their most characteristic. It is hard to think of either doing anything squalid or mean; and it is harder to think of either withdrawing her loyalty once she had given it. Inevitably perhaps, Elizabeth thought better of Ivy's novels than Ivy did of Elizabeth's; but they both had the highest regard for each other as people. They both also shared the highest regard for Robert Liddell as a writer and a friend. The relationship between the three of them was an equilateral triangle, in which no side surpassed the others in the quality or quantity of the understanding, respect and affection given and received.

Francis King

1

The following pages will give some account of my friendship with two distinguished writers, and of their friendship with each other. The title is imitated from the delightful *Ivy and Stevie* (about Ivy Compton-Burnett and Stevie Smith) by Kay Dick, though my materials are very different from hers and therefore the pattern that I shall construct from them must also be very different.

It was in the sad, wet summer of 1945. Back from Egypt for three months I was staying with my aunt in the Victorian villa in Tunbridge Wells in which we had both been born. Now it was in decay; we shifted foot-baths about on the landing to catch drips from the roof, which we could get no one to repair. Around us were the closed bedroom doors of people lately dead. Had I then known Elizabeth Taylor's work, I might have imagined her using such a setting. One day when I changed my aunt's library book for her the girl handed me *At Mrs Lippincote's*, the first novel of a new author, published that year. 'This is remarkably intelligent,' said my aunt – which is what she meant, though she would have used other words. My aunt had taste, and had perceived something new, unusual and pleasing, and when she passed the book on to me I was equally delighted. So began my long friendship with Elizabeth Taylor and her writing.

The novel is humorous rather than comic, and melancholy rather than sad, and yet entirely unsentimental: the tale of an Air Force officer (very firmly on the ground) and his mercurial wife,

Julia. In Elizabeth's third novel, *A View of the Harbour* (1947), Beth, a novelist and the first artist to appear in her work, is a woman who seldom goes out of her house, and every time she does so, it is to see the world with the new vision of a convalescent. Julia is like that too, so that some years later I asked Elizabeth if she herself looked at the world in that way. Perhaps she sometimes did, she replied – with sudden sideways glances – but she was far from being housebound. She wrote, however:

> I had not thought of catching things on the hop, as Ivy would say. I described Beth being like it, but I was not conscious of doing it myself. Perhaps I do. It has its disadvantages in one's daily life, and I remember now that I described this in At Mrs L's – how Julia was like that and her family found it tiring and annoying, because she came to everything freshly and without preconceived opinions, and wasted time and came to odd conclusions because nothing was taken for granted. I wouldn't describe anything that was not what I had gone through and understood myself – in my experience or out of my imagination and other people's words wouldn't do. I shut my eyes and tremble with the effort to get it vividly in my mind. It runs away and I pursue it till I'm worn out and nearly in tears. It never comes easily – and nothing comes just from my head. I seem to have to transplant myself bodily. That is how, I suspect, I lose the wood for the trees.

But it is very much more important for the novelist to see the trees rather than the wood.

Julia is not an artist, except in the kitchen; but she has something of her creator's buoyancy of mind, as well as her loathing of artificial sociability. She contrasts well with the solemn Eleanor, her husband's cousin and in love with him, who tries to satisfy herself emotionally by writing to a prisoner of war and by frequenting a group of left-wing people. The pattern might remind one of Julien Green, the book not at all. The people are displaced by the war, living in a hired house (Mrs Lippincote's), probably in Reading: there is a river and there are abbey ruins. Julia's devotion to the Brontë legend is a leitmotiv, and behind them all is the all-powerful Wing Commander, the 'old man', a sort of 'Mr Rochester' figure. What was he in civil life? None of the adults knows; but his small daughter reveals the horrid truth to Julia's small son. He was a dentist.

Three years later, in Egypt, I received a letter signed 'Elizabeth Taylor'. She had liked my novel, *The Last Enchantments*; in some way (the expression is hackneyed, but I can find none better) it had touched her where she lived. It is not necessarily the best books that do that, or the most famous. Sometimes you are more touched by a book that seems to belong to you alone rather than to the world. In that spirit, John Davenport, that lazy, combative and yet most perceptive of critics, wrote to me saying that he almost hoped not to have to share his pleasure in this book with too many other people.

Years later Elizabeth wrote to me: 'I felt I was participating in it, not just reading it, and what I felt wasn't just admiration. . . . Perhaps you brought out the best that was in me and I was grateful for that. It was love I felt; yes, when I have read your books I feel more loving, and it is no use being alive if one doesn't feel that.' So it was that when I was asked to contribute an account of Elizabeth Taylor's novels to a book of reference I remembered these words and wrote that her motive power was Love: 'Not the love that is a four-letter word, nor yet anything so theoretical as Christian charity, but most certainly a great virtue.' It was not even 'love of life' – that is more like it, but the phrase has come to mean many things that could (happily) not be predicated of her. She loved life indeed – but critically, fastidiously and intelligently. She loved few people, but those very much, and her love extended to inanimate objects which (I think) she much preferred to animals. She once told me that she could never commit suicide because of her curiosity about what was going to happen next. I must be thankful (and surprised) that this appetite for love and life found food in my book.

But I am sure that what determined her to write to me was this paragraph: 'The author we most admire has rightly said that people do not know about families; but Stephen and I know. It is one of the ways in which we are unlike people.' Of course she recognized the author to whom I referred as Ivy Compton-Burnett, who was not then (1948) so extensively known as she soon was to be. I do not know when Elizabeth had first fallen under the spell, but I know that her friendship with Ivy did not begin until a year or two later.

2

At this point I must go back in time to record the beginning of my own friendship with Ivy Compton-Burnett. It lasted, like that with Elizabeth, for over a quarter of a century, though the five meetings between us were all over by the autumn of 1947.

In 1935 a page by David Garnett in the *New Stateman* first introduced me to her work, and I saw that *A House and Its Head* was a book likely to give me quite peculiar pleasure. I ordered it at the branch of the Times Library then housed in Elliston and Cavell's, the nearest equivalent to Harrods in the Oxford of pre-war years, and remember with what excitement I received it from their admirable librarian Miss Lush (now Lady Ormerod) at the end of my day's work in the Bodleian. It filled a weekend when I was alone; my brother Donald, who lived with me, had gone up to London to hear the celebrated violinist Kreisler.

At first the strange staccato sentences and the inattention to euphony struck harshly on my ear, and I wondered, Can she write? Soon I was converted by the precision and subtlety, and saw that she wrote better than anyone else. By then the subject-matter had enthralled me, and I shall not say that I felt more loving. Donald and I, children of an unhappy home, had in the past found strength and consolation in such very different masters of cruel family life as Sophocles and Samuel Butler. Here was someone nearer to us who knew all the horror that can lurk behind the façade of the respectable, upper-middle-class English home. 'It's about us!' I exclaimed – as once I had exclaimed when reading the *Electra*. I read it twice, my hair (like that of Henry Tilney in *Northanger Abbey*) standing on end. I walked alone vigorously, churning it over in my mind, on our favourite Sunday walk – through Islip and Noke, over the hill to Beckley and back by Elsfield. I thought I should go mad if my brother did not come home at the appointed hour, for I longed to thrust it into his hands.

Thereafter we eagerly obtained the precious four novels of the canon and she became our favourite writer. Our talk was full of her locutions, such as 'I do not wish to be speaking of it', or 'in all the ways that don't go into words'. During our rare separations we wrote letters in her manner, whenever we could find or construct conversations to report; and I corresponded in this way with our friend, the excellent and long unjustly neglected novelist, Barbara Pym. We promptly bought the next two novels when they came out, and in the Bodleian catalogue I discovered *Dolores*, the early work of which no mention was made in the list of titles prefacing her later books. I wrote to Blackwood, the publisher, and obtained a copy at the original price of five shillings. It is now worth a sum many, many times that.

Meanwhile we longed to know more about her. Many writers inspire no personal curiosity, but in her case one felt there must be a profound and perhaps rather horrible experience behind her work, and her single-minded devotion to one theme, a theme that was so poignantly interesting to us. Donald, alas, had been dead for thirty years when Hilary Spurling published her admirable biography *Ivy when Young* and gave us the answers to our questions.

'The resources of a great library' were at my disposal; but *Burke* revealed no peers or baronets, no landed gentry called Compton-Burnett, *Crockford* listed no clergy of that name. I did find out that Noël Compton-Burnett had been a fellow of King's, and had been killed in the war. The great discovery, however, was in *The Times* index: 'Inquest on Katharine and Stephanie [Primrose] Compton-Burnett'. The back numbers of *The Times* newspaper were kept in a basement, under Radcliffe Square. I had to wait impatiently till I was free to go down there, and huddled uncomfortably among the book-stacks I turned up the page with trembling fingers. Iris Compton-Burnett (but not Ivy) was called in evidence. The pathetic story has been told, as far as it can now be known, in Mrs Spurling's book, but an element of mystery remains. Where were the two girls during the last fortnight of their lives? Did they commit suicide (and if so, why?) This strange happening in her own family must, one cannot help thinking, have influenced her future plot construction quite as much as her reading of Wilkie Collins. 'There are signs of strange things happening, though they do not emerge,' she once said. There had certainly been signs.

Apart from reviews, nothing seemed to have been written about her except for a sympathetic article by Richard Strachey in the *London Mercury*. I did not then know any literary people, and my first contact with Ivy (at one remove) was when Spencer Curtis Brown (later to become literary executor of Elizabeth Bowen and Somerset Maugham) accepted the agency of my first novel late in 1937. He said (which now surprises me) that she was very deaf and very slow. He offered to show me her photograph, but he could not find it.

In 1940 I had prepared an essay on Ivy's novels, which I had some prospect of placing in *Horizon*. Nothing came of this, and its first appearance, brought up to date, was as an appendix to my book *A Treatise on the Novel* (1947). It was no doubt a disappointment to her that this, the first serious appraisement of her work, should have been so long delayed. I ventured to write to her, offering to send my manuscript if she wished, for (as I said) it would be a pity to make mistakes about a living writer who was there to correct them. Ivy was pleased: 'I am grateful for being brought before the public,' she wrote. 'My books are very little known.' I sent her the manuscript, and she appointed a day for me to come to tea and take it back.

It was in a region well known to me. At the corner of Gloucester Road was St Stephen's Church, whose dark, incense-laden interior had once been a place of sanctuary, and will always be dear to me. *Churches are best for prayer that have least light.* . . . Then there was Cornwall Gardens. Donald and I, who as schoolboys frequented the South Kensington museums during our holidays, and returned by various routes to tea in our hated home, must often have passed that way. It is even possible that now and again an extra long detour may have caused us to walk below the windows of Braemar Mansions ('not mansions,' wrote Ivy, 'but converted out of houses'), little knowing that there sat the sibyl who would completely have understood all our troubles.

Ivy opened the door to me. She was small, neatly dressed in black, and rather surprisingly jewelled; her greying corn-coloured hair reminded me a little of the 'blond head' in the Acropolis Museum in Athens. In speech her vowels were somewhat drawn out; she would be called 'chatty'. More measured in speech and more personally impressive was her friend Margaret Jourdain, the great authority on English furniture, a younger sister of Eleanor Jourdain, sometime contentious Principal of St Hugh's College in Oxford, and famous for her 'adventure' at Versailles. She and her friend Annie Moberley believed that they had seen Marie Antoinette at the Petit Trianon; they wrote a best-selling book about it, entitled *An Adventure*, which remains, even today, the subject of dispute.

When Ivy and Margaret had gone to get their gas masks in 1939 'the girl' had asked Margaret if she were one of the heroines of *An Adventure.* Ivy went on: 'Margaret said to the girl: "No, it was my sister." "But you write too?" said the girl to her. Then she said to me: "Miss Burnett, I believe you write?" I felt quite glad that our maid didn't write too, otherwise she might also have been the subject of inquiry.'

Conversation, not only on that day, got on to *An Adventure* and would not easily get off it, though we wished to be speaking of other things. I also knew a great deal about it for, in the records room at the Bodleian, there was a tin trunk irreverently nicknamed 'Miss Jourdain's baby' by the staff. It contained a mass of papers relevant to the 'vision', and sometimes it had been my duty to show it to privileged people, though it was not for general release. Once I showed it to a psychical research woman who, after careful study of the plan of Versailles, said to me in a tense voice: 'You realize that the two ladies went *bodily* through a brick wall?' 'Oh?' I said, in what I hoped was a neutral tone. 'Why do you smile?' asked the psychical research woman. I think she must have thought that Miss Moberley and Miss Jourdain, temporarily living in the year 1789, had not been impeded by walls built after that date; but I am sure she must have misread her map.

Ivy and Margaret smiled, and we all agreed that it was remarkable that *An Adventure* had held so many people's attention for so long. I think the reason must be this: most of us have never believed that the ladies saw ghosts, and yet few of us have doubted their perfect good faith. A solution has now been offered and, if we accept it, we were right: the ladies had truthfully reported what they had seen, but in fact it was a sort of fancy-dress *fête champêtre* organized by Robert de Montesquiou: as no official permission had been granted for this, the authorities denied all knowledge of it.

I was seated on a hard sort of sofa covered with worn black velvet, and tea (as in *More Women than Men*) went 'through all its stages'. 'Watercress? Very wholesome,' offered Ivy. 'Home-made gingerbread. Very good. Cheese straws.'

The first thing she wished me to stress more fully in my essay was the goodness of many of her characters, even the occasional goodness of some of her tyrants. I remarked on the beautiful sympathy evinced in one speech by Sophia Stace (*Brothers and Sisters*) and in another by the terrible Matty (*A Family and a Fortune*). 'It's because they were intelligent,' she said, and for her there was no greater virtue than intelligence.

Margaret picked up my suggestion that some of the good characters were not sexually irreproachable. 'The doubtful Felix?' she said. 'Our landlady, when we were staying near Cambridge, said to me: "Miss Burnett must be a little naïve. That young man sitting on an old man's knee; some people would think it improper."'

'I thought it was meant to be improper,' I said.

'Oh, it was meant to be improper,' said Ivy, in a full, satisfied tone. She went on to say: 'One cut out a scene, because one didn't want trouble.'

I have wondered ever since what that scene could have been. I suspect that it took place between Felix and Gabriel, the son of his elderly lover, Jonathan Swift. Rereading *More Women than Men*, I ask myself each time whether the relations between them are suggested with extreme subtlety, or whether something is lacking.

I asked Ivy if she owed anything to Greek tragedy. I have always remembered her as saying 'One came between brothers and shared their tutor' as an explanation of her knowledge of Greek. I must have got it wrong, for 'one' was older than the two brothers, Guy and Noël. Greek tragedy showed one, she said, that things could happen.

My only other question, I think, was about the 'silent years', between *Dolores* (1911) and *Pastors and Masters* (1925).

'One was a good deal cut up by the war,' she answered. 'One's brother was killed, and one had family troubles.'

To me, remembering the extraordinary deaths of Katharine and Primrose, in bed together with a copy of Trine's *In Tune with the Infinite* open between them, this seemed a masterly understatement.

There followed a long talk about books. Perhaps we began on Elizabeth Bowen's *The Death of the Heart*. Ivy spoke with slight sardonic amusement but without envy – without, that is, grudging envy – of Elizabeth Bowen's success. 'I suppose her publisher sends her peaches,' she remarked. And: 'I hear people are always writing to her about the deaths of *their* hearts.' Ivy would have enjoyed the peaches, but not the letters.

I said that I felt, uncomfortably, that the poor little heroine of that book had been more cruelly betrayed by her author than by her heartless elders.

'Not a genial book,' said Ivy with approval.

We ranged over miscellaneous novels. Both of us loved *The Heir of Redclyffe* by Charlotte Yonge. I told her that an aunt of mine used to insist that Charles, the crippled brother in the book, was secretly in love with his cousin, Lady Eveleen. I could find nothing in the text to justify such an idea, but my aunt said she knew by 'feminine intuition'.

'There's no such thing,' said Ivy firmly; and as, if feminine intuition existed, she above all women would have been gifted with it, I think we must believe her.

Her passion for Jane Austen, of course, had been revealed to me by her own writing. 'Once I felt I should go mad because I couldn't finish *The Watsons*.' She also talked lovingly about Dickens: 'I don't know how often I've read the Marshalsea scenes in *Little Dorrit*.' She did not bother about the rest of the book. I told her how much I disliked Katherine Mansfield as a personality, and she faintly rebuked me: 'What I feel is that we should be so *grateful* to her.'

Some weeks later my brother and I were passing through London, and I asked if I might bring him to see her. It was a hurried occasion, as we were all going to catch a train: the same train, as it turned out, for Donald and I were going home to Oxford, and Ivy and Margaret were going with Herman Schrijver – the Dutch interior decorator who became the closest of her men friends – to spend a week at Woodstock, and walk in the park at Blenheim. Ivy remarked: 'Rose Macaulay asked me if I were a good walker and I said I was. I meant three miles there and back with sandwiches, she meant twenty miles.'

I fancy Ivy thought out bits of her books when walking. Once she said: 'I don't know what I should do without Kensington Gardens.'

Tea hurriedly went through some of its stages, and unfortunately *An Adventure* came up again. 'What those ladies said isn't evidence,' said Ivy trenchantly, to the delight of Donald, who was fond of the Law. We parted at Paddington, and assured them that they would have to change trains at Oxford. They did not believe us, and were carried on to Banbury.

During their stay in Woodstock they came to tea with us in our flat in the Banbury Road. I quote from my account of it in a letter to Elizabeth, ten years later: it will be seen that I am answering her questions.

They made a short visit, I suspect that they were going on to M.J.'s [Margaret Jourdain's] brother and like Dulcia [in *A House and Its Head*] expected to come by a good deal of refreshment in the course of their peregrinations. I poured out, and they wanted a lot of water in their tea (we also drank China tea, but liked it strong). Tea went through all its stages – scones (I fancy), gingerbread (which was a success), and small cakes with chopped walnut on which were rather good, but I don't think they appealed to her – she hasn't a sweet tooth, I think. . . . They were punctual to a minute, so we didn't hang out of the window – anyway the view on the roadside was very constricted, as far as arriving people were concerned. I had a sprained ankle, so if there was any last-minute shopping Donald would have done it – but I think it is unlikely: he was far too efficient and well-balanced to have forgotten anything.

M.J. talked a lot, and Donald said I encouraged her too much, and that I.C.B. was on the point of being more personal and interesting if I had let her – but I was rather shy of it.

They walked to the window and gazed with interest at the North Oxford back gardens, and their flowering trees. I.C.B. was interested in our neighbours – particularly a large family that lived upstairs at the time.

But the whole incident was less memorable than it should have been – she seemed like an ordinary human being, very neat in a coat and skirt, talking about her hotel at Woodstock.

'Everything seemed to come out of tins – except the boiled chicken, they could hardly tin that.' But Donald thought they could.

*

I had mentioned that neighbours of ours had had a difference with Colonel Jourdain.

'Henry was always a very disagreeable boy,' said Margaret.

Clumsily, I had described the difference as a 'feud', though it was only of short duration.

'Then it wasn't a feud,' Ivy corrected me.

None of us spoke of the war, in which (I think) none of us much believed; but it was there all the time like a nagging pain. Soon, my brother and I knew, it must separate us, and we lived these last months together in the mutual kindness that (I hope and imagine) commonly exists between deeply attached people of whom one has been condemned by the doctors – but we might both be condemned. Such a time seems happier than it was in recollection, for anxiety, its chief torment, is over. Anxiety may be replaced by loss and intolerable grief, but at least it does not in itself last for ever – not even in hell, where there is no hope.

It was in 1945 that I came back to England after five years' absence in Greece and Egypt. During that long, wet summer I had two painful tasks. Donald (an airborne orderly in the RAMC) had died of wounds in Normandy a year before, and I had to dismantle our flat in Oxford. Most of my time, however, was spent in Tunbridge Wells. My aunt, the last survivor of my mother's family, had lost her sister the previous year, and I helped her to arrange for the sale of most of the contents of her house, and for her own establishment in a club. She had a cook and a gardener, but they were both senile and mad, and of little use to us. In the horrible long light evenings (double summer time) I went through my brother's papers.

During this time I revisited Braemar Mansions. It was a comparatively fine day, and a table was drawn up to the window. Sour milk was hanging up in muslin, to turn into cream cheese.

'Marge?' offered Ivy, in a frank, open tone, and tea went through such stages as could be managed in those days of austerity.

I wished that I had written to the two women about Donald's death, and that I was not now obliged to tell them of it.

Ivy was flustered. She was very much upset, for her own life had been 'smashed up' by the deaths of her brothers. 'Oh, dear!' she said. 'That's bad news. I hadn't heard.'

Margaret was socially far more adequate.

They had enjoyed my *Watering-Place*, a collection of interlinked sketches about Tunbridge Wells, lately published ('We'd been rather badly off for books'), and they had tales of other writers.

Edith Sitwell had wanted to sue a reviewer because his notice was likely to hurt the sales of her book – and we thought it had merely been his duty to his readers to discourage them from buying a book that he thought bad. Dame Una Pope-Hennessy (the formidable mother of James and John Pope-Hennessy and a friend of Ivy and Margaret) had been cross with a reviewer who had written of her book about jade: 'Dame Una skirts gracefully round the subject.'

'I don't know why one should know about jade,' said Ivy. 'I only know that it's the green stuff that comes from China.'

'I know a great deal more about it than that,' said Margaret, in a full, satisfied voice.

During my next two years' absence in Egypt *Manservant and Maidservant* appeared (1947). I wrote to tell Ivy of my delight in it, and of a sense of frustration in being unable to share this pleasure with my brother. As a mark of gratitude I sent her a food parcel which, she was good enough to say, miraculously filled the worst gaps in her store-cupboard. I have never known which of them did the catering. I knew that in 1945 they could not make do on their rations.

In the following August I was in England again, and went again to Braemar Mansions. We had tea in the dining-room, a depressing room which looked into a court. Margaret came in latish, bringing ice-cream, for which Ivy and I were insufficiently grateful, I am afraid. Ivy caught me alone in the passage to say how much I must miss Donald. 'Dreadfully,' I said, and it was very much worse when I was in England. This she well understood, though she did not think much of 'Abroad'. But I remained

'Abroad' ever since. I never ran away, but stayed away.

She spoke of a near-relation of my own: 'Do you like her?'

'Well, she's not a person one can really *dis*like.'

'But do you *like* her?'

'No.'

And Ivy beamed with approval. She knew about families.

But she did not know about religion. She spoke crossly of people who had criticized her clergymen. Oscar Jekyll (in *A House and Its Head*) cheerfully acquiesced in his sister's marriage with a divorced man, and Ernest Bellamy (in *Men and Wives*) divorced one woman and was preparing to marry another. Critics said this was impossible at the end of the nineteenth century.

'But they don't really *know*,' said Ivy.

I thought they did, but dared not say so.

My *Treatise on the Novel*, with a long essay on Ivy's novels, appeared just as I was leaving England, and she wrote her gratitude to me in Egypt. Next year I had a copy of *The Last Enchantments* sent to her, a book full of my life in Oxford with my brother. She was 'enchanted' she said, and wrote touchingly: 'It gives the measure of what you have had, and what you have lost.' And she kindly remembered how 'the two of us' had gone to tea with 'the two of you'.

Meanwhile my novel brought me other letters: from dear Father D'Arcy, an old friend; from Francis King, later to be a friend and colleague; and from Elizabeth Taylor.

3

It is not often that I receive 'fan'-letters, and I always acknowledge them unless they are impertinent, or have obviously been written by lunatics. I should in any case have answered Elizabeth's kind little note, but a reference to Ivy at once warmed me towards her. I believe that she had, as she said, seen every point that I had wished to make, and had laughed and cried at the right places.

In return she sent me her third and latest novel, *A View of the Harbour*: and it was then that I recognized her as the author of *At Mrs Lippincote's*. She firmly corrected those, including myself, who unwittingly referred to her book as *A View from the Harbour*. No, we were to look at the houses round the small port, and at their inhabitants. There was an ill-adjusted widow, and an amateur painter who gave her inadequate comfort; there was a Rabelaisian cripple, paralysed from the waist down. Most memorable was Tory, haughtily holding her very intelligent head in the air, but missing her husband, who had left her for a 'woman officer'. Next door was her school friend Beth Cazabon, the doctor's wife and a writer.

Like Julia, in the earlier book, Beth catches things 'on the hop' – almost as a student whose mind is more imaginative than philosophical will react to a first reading of Bishop Berkeley by quickly turning his head, hoping to witness the sudden appearance or disappearance of those external objects which are supposed to depend on his perception of them for their existence. Unlike Julia, she is not at all domestic, for she is plunged in her writing – as other novelists might wish to be. Compassionate and relentless as God (in whom she does not believe), she sends her creatures forth and calls them home, having (like Thomas Hardy) a love for funerals, although she has never been to one.

Tory, no novelist, provides the criticism a novelist may sometimes make of himself: 'Writers are ruined people. . . . When anything important happens you're stunned, and thrown out for a while, and then you recover . . . God, how novelists recover! . . . and you begin to wonder how you can make use of it with a little shifting here, and a little adding there, something can be made of it, surely?' Other people say things of this kind enviously, and even unkindly – novelists seem to attract the envy and unkindness of other people (though so little enviable); it is a pity they are not nicer to one another. Elizabeth's friend Maud must have said something of this sort, for I find I once wrote to her: 'Maud was right, I think. Novelists relive and reshape the past, and do more for themselves than psychiatrists could do for them, and at such vast expense. One doesn't mind anything past – only present consequences (e.g. the absence of people, resulting from their death).'

Tory also makes the other common complaint that the novelist knows less than anyone else what is in fact going on around him – he wants to make a satisfactory pattern, and hardly cares if it corresponds to anything outside his mind. Nevertheless, one would like to read the results of Beth's cerebrations; they would probably be unlike those of her creator, for Elizabeth's death roll is not long.

The correspondence between Elizabeth and me, begun in that autumn of 1948, was to become increasingly frequent and intimate, and it lasted to within a month of Elizabeth's death, when she was no longer able to hold a pen.

Elizabeth's earliest letters have been lost. They were among many things that disappeared after I left Cairo in 1953, not knowing that I should not return. It is a pity, for these were, on the whole, happy years for us both. For her, there were the children growing up, for both of us there was work, and for me that Egypt for which many of us who have known it feel a perpetual nostalgia. I must early have realized that it was to be a regular correspondence, for I kept her letters, though I usually destroy letters as soon as I have answered them. Gradually we built up a common world, partly based on the great of the past, like Jane Austen, partly on Ivy. There were private jokes, 'pretty severe philippics' against some living authors and critics, and – out of her own surroundings – the introduction of some wonderful 'flat' characters whose utterance could never fail to delight. They deserve the same immortality as Dorothy Osborne's tiresome old suitor or Madame de Sévigné's boring Breton neighbours, but Elizabeth in her charity has spared them this.

From early on we had destined our letters to destruction. In 1957, by a coincidence, we both sorted letters and set them in order. I wrote that I had done so before going to Athos.

> There must be more in Cairo under 'sequestration'. I have about a pound and a half in a gigantic envelope . . . I endorsed them to be returned to you, should a shark eat me. If it didn't, I thought re-reading had better keep for a rainy day. I had done a little Cassandra Austen editing in the past, destroying a few. . . . Perhaps you would like to do something similar with mine – but just as you prefer. Think how Miss X [an author whom, in jest, we feared as our editress] would like to edit the whole correspondence if we predecease her. Do we leave out dates to fox her? I have never known. Perhaps we should take further precautions – or outlive her. 'That will be the best and the most difficult way.' (*Pastors and Masters*)

Elizabeth's mind on the subject was very clear to me. I know that after the suicide of her friend Maud Geddes she destroyed all Maud's letters, and all her own when they were sent back to her.

Later we were both shocked (as Ivy was) by the betrayal of Rose Macaulay by her literary executor, who published some of her intimate correspondence, and Elizabeth remarked how coy and silly letters could look when seen out of context. We both detested Katherine Mansfield and her whining, coarse letters, and we were aware that our private jokes and Ivyisms would look no better to outsiders than her Dickensianisms and her 'my strikes!'. We were, on the whole, comparatively fortunate people but, like everyone else, we had our anxieties and sorrows; and, friends as we were, it was natural that we should communicate them to one another although, like well-mannered people, we wrote letters mainly intended to give pleasure. Neither of us need say

> My pen's the spout
> Where the rainwater of mine eyes runs out.

Nevertheless, in the course of the years, there were some letters that were painful, and meant for no other eyes; and no other eyes will see them.

Late in 1970 Hilary Spurling wrote to me to ask for help in her book on Ivy. I wrote to Elizabeth:

> I mentioned you among the people she should contact, simply that. She does not know (and shall not unless you reveal it) that I have your records of Braemar conversations. I have looked out some, and they are marvellous. I thought . . . of getting photostats done. Then you could edit them for her, if you feel you are willing for her to use them. . . . I think you could obliterate or cut out easily – what do you think? Of course if you are against it in principle, that is an end of it (and there has been no beginning).

Elizabeth said she would like to see copies of these letters, and she gave them to Mrs Spurling – this, I think, justifies the presence of Braemar letters here.

Early in 1975, when the condition of her health – she had had a recurrence of cancer – was obviously very serious, Elizabeth wrote to me about the letters, requesting the destruction of her own after her death, and asking what I wished to be done with mine. I said I wished mine to be destroyed, but asked if I might keep some of hers of a literary interest. 'I rather hope I may get those concerned to invite me to do you in the Authors and their Work series – though I haven't done anything about it – I might then like to quote a bit or two out of a letter (e.g. about Ivy), but I devoutly hope you will be able to censor the thing for yourself' – for there was still hope, or I was allowed to think so. Elizabeth answered that she particularly did not want anything to remain that might hurt any living person among her friends – and so with one blow she destroyed the 'flat' characters, who could have given her a second literary fame. But she allowed the continued existence of 'literary' letters. I most scrupulously carried out my promise to her, despite the dishonest if well-meant advice of various people who suggested that I should deposit her letters in a great library. I know about great libraries and their ways, having worked in one.

Later, to my surprise, I heard that my own letters were still in existence. She had told me that I might rely on their destruction, but the note which she left directing this had become deeply embedded among them. Her husband kindly returned them to me, and I was able to do a great deal of destruction for myself.

4

Gradually Elizabeth and I got to know each other; Elizabeth already knew something of me from *The Last Enchantments*. I learned that, like Jane Austen, she was an ASROG (Abbey School Reading Old Girl), though it was not until years later that she sent me these scraps from a diary kept during her schooldays.

We went to see *Antigone* in Greek but although we were well primed beforehand you can't follow it without a crib. Peggy made quite a good joke. She leant across and said, 'This is all Greek to me.' I thought we should die of laughing, but soon sobered up on seeing Miss T.'s hurt expression, because I daresay she can take it in her stride all right. She certainly looked quite excited, like the day when we went to hear Professor Gilbert Murray, and he let his subject run away with him. . . .

I loathe Virgil. We did all the part about bile. Hilary looked sick while she was construing, and Miss B. said she was tired of our affectations. . . .

All the time Miss B. was rowing me I thought 'Dire was the twang of his silver bow' out of Iliad Six, and she said 'I'm surprised you think it a smiling matter.'

On the last passage Elizabeth noted: 'Could this have been the Queen of Ithaca?' We had both been participants in the Prime of Miss Sylvia Benton, the distinguished archaeologist who was

in Athens in the early sixties. Sylvia had taught Ancient Greek to
Elizabeth, and Modern Greek to me: dire indeed would have been
the twang.

I went to hear Baldwin at the Town Hall. I must say it was an
awful lot of rot, although we had reserved seats. . . .

If those brothers in Comus had really been anxious about
their sisters would they have stood around spouting poetry? All
the same, Sabrina Fair is heavenly and rather like some of the
poetry Deirdre wrote last summer. . . .

In English, Miss J. was telling us about the Blessed
Damozel. I said it was interesting how Rossetti buried his
poems in his wife's grave because he was so upset. And then
wanted to publish them and dug them up and the body was in a
frightful state of decomposition and some of the hair came away
with the poems. While I was speaking, Miss J. looked out of the
window in a sarcastic manner and when I had finished she said
'thank you' very politely but with rather a sneering look. I think
she thought I had taken the wind out of Rossetti's sails. . . .

I am reading Freud. It only seems to be things I know
already. . . .

On my last day at school
Everyone else knows what they are going to do, except me.
This evening I tried to read some of *Alcestis*, but it wasn't the
same. I feel as if my life is over, and I don't know what to do.
Perhaps someone will marry me. In the meantime I have started
another novel.

Our 'disembodied friendship', as she called it, grew. I read of
her collecting ivy with her children for Christmas decorations (she
rightly hated holly), while I told her of walks by the Nile with
Sappho, my pretty mongrel bitch, watching the beautiful boats
with big-bellied sails bringing cattle-fodder from Upper Egypt.

And of course we searched each for the other's books. Her

second novel, *Palladian* (1946), is short, formal, beautifully designed. I told her: 'This is almost my favourite kind [of book] – when someone goes to a decaying country house, and finds a lot of odd people in it. Almost the most horrifying predicament in life, but so entertaining in fiction.'

The heroine, Cassandra Dashwood (obviously an ASROG), goes to such a house to be a governess, and fulfils her Jane Eyre dreams of falling in love with and marrying her employer, the scholarly Marion Vanbrugh. Aunt Tinty, an amiable half-wit, keeps house for him and sings sentimental songs in the gloaming; her daughter, Margaret, is a heavily pregnant, rather mannish woman doctor whose husband is far away; her son, Tom, is an eternal and drunken medical student, engaged in a squalid affair with the woman at the village pub. Over them all, and especially over the little pupil Sophy, broods the ghost of the brilliant and beautiful Violet, Sophy's mother. After Sophy's pathetic death Tom confesses that he was really her father, and Violet's ghost is laid.

This is a distinguished, elegant book, almost more 'Gothic' in style than Palladian, with the lunatic old Nanny, the collapsing conservatory, dismembered statuary, and all the cruel vagaries of the English weather: rain drips down the windows 'like gin'.

However, it was in her fourth novel, *A Wreath of Roses* (1949), that Elizabeth really arrived. Years later she told me that she did not like that book, and I do not know if that were due to a momentary impatience with it or if (as I hope it was not) it was a permanent feeling of dissatisfaction, for it seems to me so beautiful. Here, for the first time, her visual powers are fully exploited, and her exquisite taste in painting. Her most interesting character is an elderly painter, Frances Rutherford. This dialogue between her and her admirer, Morland Beddoes, is most significant – it deserves to be a *locus classicus* of criticism, and gives the final justification for Elizabeth's sort of art:

'I committed a grave sin against the suffering of the world

by ignoring it, by tempting others with charm and nostalgia until they ignored it too.'

'By looking at one thing, we must always ignore another.'

'How stuffy it is in here!' She was busy lighting a lamp. As the blue coronet of flame reached upwards, her hands guarding it looked transparent.

'I always felt,' she said, 'that life's not worth living, that I could only contemplate little bits of it and keep my sanity; and those bits I selected carefully – the sun on a breakfast-table, girls dressing, flowers . . .'

'But it wasn't all happy. Sadness often looked out of those girls' eyes.'

'An English sadness. Delicious to contemplate.'

'The picture of Liz on the sofa – she was a woman alone in a room; as only God, I should have thought, could possibly have seen her. It was the truth.'

'All *little* things,' she said impatiently, blowing out a match.

'But *not* little. That *is* life. It's loving-kindness and simplicity, and it lay all the time in your pictures, implicit in every petal and every jug you ever painted.'

It is Morland Beddoes who is right, and he gives the answer to those who have called Elizabeth's work 'trivial'; it *is* life. For him the girl in the picture 'was made to seem perfectly in context as he had never been able to see people before'. That picture 'turned life a little under his very eyes . . . all, through Frances's eyes, could be made static and beautiful and set in a pattern'. This is, indeed, one of the highest functions of art to bring order out of chaos, and 'charity, delight, increase' out of disorder. Thus messy Liz Corbett, the painter in *The Soul of Kindness* (1964), was 'creatively orderly'. Art must select to make its patterns, and must ignore what it cannot use; and it can use a great deal.

Frances, like her creator, is – whether consciously or not – a realist. She can set something or someone perfectly in context; she can see bits of life steadily instead of trying to see it whole, when it is intolerable. Her pictures are truth and are beauty, whatever pain or ugliness may lie outside. For some people, as for Morland Beddoes, they will make life more endurable.

The relations between the three women, Frances and her guests Liz and Camilla, are exquisitely done. Liz is married, uneasily rather than unhappily, and trying to make her way as a young mother without impairing her friendship with Camilla. And Camilla is unhappily involved in a sexual attraction towards a worthless stranger, who is in fact a murderer hiding from justice. Her aberration (and as such she clearly sees it) destroys her peace, and puts a wall between her and her friends. Fortunately she will be shaken out of it with violence.

This book may well have shown Elizabeth her powers and her limitations. Her murderer is unreal compared with Elizabeth Bowen's Prothero in her short story 'The Disinherited'. But the world of the women is real through and through, and so are their appendages. Frances has a horrible dog, Hotchkiss, the most odious and also the most convincing dog in literature. She has also a splendid charwoman. Liz has a clerical husband, who owns a car like a tin bath, displays an oar on his study wall, and writes notes to his more important lady parishioners with frequent recourse to the *Dictionary of Quotations*. She has also a teething baby, *pinched* and *veined* and smelling of milk.

It was about this time that Elizabeth's growing reputation began to attract the envy and malice of reviewers. 'Feminine, feminine!' cried the manlier sort of lady novelist. But we may be glad that she decided to be feminine, as thus she was made. Compton Mackenzie truly said that while it is easy for a woman to behave like a man, it is impossible for her to behave like a gentleman. This is true of writing as well as of other activities. It seems unfair, since *Howards End* proves that a man can write like a perfect lady, if a trifle bourgeoise. (I once knew an elderly diplomat who had been much annoyed as a young man because he was suspected of having written under the pen-name of 'E.M. Forster';

he would very much have preferred to be thought the author of dull, upper-class novels, like those of Maurice Baring.)

It was also at this time that Elizabeth was first invited to a 'very *simple* luncheon' at Braemar Mansions. I think it was the result of a fan-letter. Ivy found her very elegant and said of her (I am told): 'She's a young woman who looks as if she had never had to wash her gloves.' And yet Ivy had had a far more prosperous early life.

It was in those days, when Margaret was still alive, that I gave my former colleague Peter Duval-Smith – whose private life and whose work as an academic journalist always seemed to be equally chaotic – the introduction to Braemar Mansions that he so much wanted. I bought a large box of loukoumi for him to take, to ensure him a good reception.

Conversation, so he told me, as so often at the Mansions, was about Rose Macaulay. 'She's writing about ruins, not just ordinary ruins, but things made to look like ruins. I don't know what she sees in them.'

Margaret and Peter pursued the subject, and Ivy began to whisper, but unusually loudly: 'I don't know why Margaret is showing off like this. She can't realize how silly she sounds. And this young man knows nothing about it at all.'

Finally Margaret showed him out, saying at the door: 'What do you think of Edith Sitwell's poetry? We think it bosh.'

Peter said that he too was very much of that opinion, and Margaret cried joyfully: 'Ivy! Ivy! Come here! This young man says Edith Sitwell's poems are bosh.'

5

One of Elizabeth's readers, she told me, had rightly deduced that she was a good cook. This gave us a further topic for conversation for, I hope, it might have been said of us (in Demetrios Capetanakis's famous line): 'They were so nice, and interested in cooking.'

Years later she told me that she had regretted that I did not include some of his mother's receipts in my life of Cavafy. Elizabeth's handwriting is as beautiful and legible as that of Harícleia Cavafy is crabbed and hideous, so it is one of hers that I now copy out:

Daube à la Montigny-en-Vexin

Jean-Jacques Rousseau
Elizabeth Taylor

3 lbs tender beef

You can use topside if you are short of money, but fillet is better of course. I don't know if you know your joints.
(Note – this knowledge would be of no use to me in Greece, where no butcher knows them.)
a thick slice of ham
a calf's foot split in half (or a pig's trotter would do).
Chop ham with large onion and a large carrot (very fine). Put this at the bottom of a deep casserole, which must not be much bigger than the piece of meat, which you should then put in

with the calf's foot on top. Then a tiny amount of rosemary – only two or three of those spiky leaves, and a bay leaf and a little basil. Pour over it a liquid made of half dry white wine and half water. The dish should fit the meat so well that it doesn't take too much liquid to just cover the meat. A little salt and pepper. Put the lid on the casserole and then cover again with greaseproof paper bound round the lid so that the dish is quite sealed. Cook *very slowly* for six hours. When cool, take out the calf's foot. . . . Skim fat off dish, every scrap. This is terribly important. Next day, turn out the meat in its jelly and eat it. It is a change from the Provençal Daube because the meat is kept whole. It is simpler to cook. I forgot to say take out the bay leaf before it sets.

Of course we were fascinated by revolting food, and liked inventing horror meals. I told her of that woman novelist who made a character in Provence ladle out onion soup, followed by bouillabaisse for *luncheon*, and in summer too. Elizabeth completed the terrible menu with *tripes à la mode de Caen* and *crème brûlée*.

In *A Game of Hide-and-Seek* (1951) the food is very nasty. We begin with the nut cutlets of a vegetarian household where Harriet and Vesey meet as adolescents. When life brings them into touch again twenty years later, and they are hopelessly in love, a climactic scene takes place in an inferior tea-shop which they visit during a furtive day together in London. The setting is nearly as horrible as the inn-parlour in *Great Expectations* – and each is perhaps more acutely in love than any character in English fiction since Pip. Vesey slowly unrolls a stale Chelsea bun; and it is to be feared he is hungry enough to eat it. It is the 'objective correlative' of their love and pain.

'Harriet thought of the drinking in bars, lingering in tea-shops, railway-stations, benches in parks; in streets under a dark building, in the darkest place between two lamps. The course of unlawful love never does run smooth; or with dignity; or with romance.' And yet in the intensity of their feeling, mixed with memories of early youth, there is a beauty – and the author has spared them sordidness, one feels, by never letting their love run its full course. It was part of its essence that it should be frustrated. Elizabeth was not quite satisfied with the end of the book. Once I expressed regret that Vesey should be marked for death, and she said it was 'the kindest thing'. This remark was so uncharacteristic of her that I am sure it was fully meant.

Nevertheless the book is in places gloriously funny. Harriet works for a time in a 'gown-shop' and takes part in the rather gruesome beauty treatment of the other 'sales-ladies'. Mrs Curzon, her 'lady-cleaner', is in the great tradition of comic servants, always so well done in this author's work. So are her romantic schoolgirls, and Betsy in this book is the most imaginative of all the race. It is her ambition to be tried for her life for murdering a small tobacconist with a meat-cleaver, only to be dramatically cleared when her alibi is established by the bishop who was confirming her at the very moment of the crime. For one schoolmistress she writes an ASROG sort of essay on the exhumation of Rossetti's poems, and she informs another that 'Vesey is really her father'.

It was in April that year that Margaret Jourdain died, rather unexpectedly, after an operation. I wrote to Ivy (more or less): 'People say that work is a comfort at such times, and I have always thought it very sad that an author's work is no good at all, and indeed cannot be done.' 'You, if anyone, can understand,' she replied, and agreed that work could not even be thought of. To Elizabeth she wrote that life seemed to have been torn away. To every invitation or suggestion Ivy returned the heart-breaking phrase 'I should enjoy that later', and evidently never expected again to enjoy anything at all. But in time the phrase turned into an excellent formula of excuse, and Elizabeth and I could use it with no feeling of heartlessness. I told her that once, going into church, I had seen a kind young priest christening a very nice baby. 'Marie-Antoinette, veux-tu être baptisée?' he asked. Her ear-splitting howls said clearly: 'I should enjoy that later.'

For both of us pen and ink was probably the best means of communication, being the tools of our trade. We were not so very much alike. She cared for religion as little as I for politics – less, for politics painfully makes itself heard and felt; twice it came near to breaking up my life, even though I defied it to interest me. I know nothing of modern painting, I have seen so little, and it was her passion. She (for no one is perfect) cared nothing for Dickens, and hardly read French at all. But we had a great deal of literature in common, and a love of landscape; we thought (Dickens excepted) the same things funny; and we had some similar slants of vision. We both cared very much for very few people. She might have agreed with my friend Roger Hinks – who, after his unmerited disgrace over the too energetic cleaning of the Elgin Marbles, left the British Museum to work for years for the British Council – that the compensation for having acquaintances is that we can make game of them with our friends. But she would have taken more pains than I (and far more than Roger) not to hurt them. I think I may say with Dryden:

> Sure our souls were near ally'd; and thine
> Cast in the same Poetick mould with mine.
> One common Note on either Lyre did strike,
> And knaves and Fools we both abhorr'd alike.

In March 1953 I received the last of her novels to reach me in Egypt.

It arrived [I wrote] at the end of an appalling day of Khamseen – a would-be pergola and a trellis came crashing down on my roof-top, overturning my palms and wrecking my aspidistras. I have never bought an aspidistra in my life, and I don't know how they accumulate on the roof – offerings, perhaps, from the garden-boy who looks after it?

After all the banging and crashing, and the stifling oppression that goes with it, *The Sleeping Beauty* was a comfort and delight:

it could not have been better timed. . . . I lived in the book, as in your others: I liked particularly Isabella and Evalie, and their gay early middle age – how comforting, too, to be with people who find 'the Change' such fun, when one thinks of the depressing nonsense that most people make out of it. . . . If I faintly wish Isabella had had some intellectual interests – and she could have been very funny about them – am I perhaps wrong? But I am so fond of the people in *A Wreath of Roses* and have so lately re-read it, that I am perhaps tiresomely asking you to do the same thing again.

Isabella's situation as a tragic widow is soon forgotten in a charming world of women's friendship: secret betting on the races, and exhausting attempts to lose weight. Equally funny is her son Laurence, doing his military service, whose deft seduction of a nursemaid would probably be as useful and practical a guide to intending seducers as the famous chapters in *Le Rouge et le Noir*. (Elizabeth said that she was not quite sure whether she ought to be pleased when I told her this; but I am sure she was pleased.)

This is her slightest book, apart from *A View of the Harbour* – though not the least amusing. The sleeping beauty herself, woken out of lifelessness by an amiable middle-aged 'prince', is sufficiently there, but not much more. They are bigamously married, and probably live happily ever after. I do not know if this triumphant wrongdoing owes anything to the example set by Ivy in *Elders and Betters*, by which I am conscious of having been influenced myself.

More important is the long-short story 'Hester Lilly'; it is far richer in atmosphere and more profound in its study of human nature. Here the great house is not crumbling, as in *Palladian*, but has suffered the worse humiliation of being perverted into a preparatory school for boys: it is divided by baize doors and encircled by cinder paths. This is the scene of the married life of Muriel, the headmaster's wife, ruined by her unnecessary jealousy of his young cousin and secretary, Hester. Muriel is perhaps this

author's most disagreeable character, though she is not seen
without pity. Hester, driven to seek friends, makes contact with
the eccentric old drunkard Miss Despenser, the last member of the
old family to which the great house originally belonged. The
squalors of Miss Despenser's cottage, and the contrasts in the house
– part house, part school – made it an appropriately visual story
for a television play.

6

Now the letters begin, those of earlier years having disappeared in Cairo. The first preserved is dated 10 June 1953; afterwards we rarely dated our letters. At this time I was in Istanbul, commissioned by Jonathan Cape to write a book about it. 'What a traveller you are!' wrote Ivy on a postcard. Elizabeth said that the place was full of letters she had written to someone who had died and had never received them. 'I was in a fine state of disintegration when I arrived for luncheon,' she wrote, about a visit to Braemar Mansions.

It is impossible in these Coronation days to judge how long it will take to get from place to place and I asked the taxi-driver not to be too early. He put me down in the Brompton Road – very kind and understanding – saying 'If you walk from here, you'll keep him waiting just a minute like all you ladies do.' I made him take me on a bit farther at the risk of him thinking I lacked the right sexual tactics. Then I was afraid I was late. I began to run, with my arms full of flowers from the garden – people stared. 'The servant' looked at me contemptuously. *She* was reading the Daily Telegraph. The room looked the same. She was pleased with the flowers and said, as I remembered her saying before – 'Before I do anything else I will give them a drink.' She looked smaller, but not much changed. Do you remember the dusty black velvet chairs and the sofa with too many cushions? There were no Coronation decorations. ('We seem to have been crowning her for a whole year. I was bored with it long ago, and so relieved to know it is really done at last.') We were alone. The longest time I have ever been alone with her. We had sherry. ('Do have some more. There is only a bottle of beer in the dining-room.') She obviously waited for me to prove myself an old toper, but I did not. She talked incessantly, her head averted towards the window-boxes. She seemed much gayer, much less strange, younger (but not in appearance), rather mischievous. We could talk about everything, but not the Five Chapters.[1] This was made clear.

Luncheon: Hot gammon, cabbage, sauté potatoes. Raspberry fool with dollops of cream. And then, oh dear, a Camembert of a mahogany colour. It had gone through all its stages. Not helped by: 'So delicious to eat, but it makes the whole flat smell as if the drains were wrong.' She was wonderfully kind and maternal to me, as she has once or twice been before. She gave me all the blobs of cream on the raspberry fool, as if I were a child.

We discussed you – 'Robert' – and your works. How once she and Margaret had tea in Oxford with you and your brother and – again – how cut up you were at his death. She was very nice about this. Of your books – 'I liked the last novel[2] very much. That old homosexual really *was* one – not like Angus Wilson's – he just says they are and we must take his word for it.'

'I wish writers would not write such annoying letters to me. Joyce Carey wrote a very kind letter. . . . I was quite glad to have it . . . sending a copy of my book to be signed, and saying he would like to have it back quickly as at least a dozen people were waiting to borrow it. . . . Such a dreadfully stupid thing

[1] A rough draft of what was to be my book on Ivy Compton-Burnett (Gollancz, 1955).
[2] *Unreal City*. 'That old homosexual' was based on the Alexandrian Greek poet Cavafy.

for one author to say to another. I always write my friends'
books into my Harrods list, even if they give me a copy, and
then I keep it out quite a time so that other people can't have it.
Another thing, is the way others think they can have free
copies. One has to pay two thirds, and Mr Gollancz only gives
me six (How many does Mr Davies give you? Exactly!). One
has one or two friends who must be given a copy, and there it
must end. And of course one must keep one or two clean copies
for an emergency.' (I love that – I hope I remember her words
correctly. I am not a good Boswell.)

We talked about horses quite a lot. How they always love her
and keep nudging her. ('Of course, one falls over, unless one is
standing against a wall.') 'I used to ride, but I can't afford it
now, naturally.' Cats she hates – all domestic animals – cannot
bear a house where there is a dog. 'Parrots are jealous.' She
loves pigs. (A wonderful categorical conversation.)

Literary: Reading life of Gorki – all Russians are brutal,
except Tchekov. 'People dislike his plays as they are all about
nothing. *I* like them very much.' She also likes Arsakov – and
that beautiful Chronicles of a Russian Family.

Rosamond's novel[3] [she called her 'Rosamond', but was only
introduced to her once at a party]. 'Little bits of it very well
written.'

Over coffee, we discussed Blanche Knopf. [For a time Alfred
Knopf published both Ivy and Elizabeth in the States.] 'I went to
see her at Claridge's . . . they are always so obsequious when
one asks for her. . . . I think I caught her on the hop, for she was
wearing trousers and sandals and . . . no, I cannot remember
what else. . . . Whatever one wears with trousers . . . she must
have worn something . . . a blouse, do you think, or jumper?
Yes, I think I caught her on the hop. I imagine she was resting
and over-ran her time. I do not understand Americans, and she
is a Jewess as well, so there you are. She said: "I think I am

[3] Rosamond Lehmann.

making a mistake about Liz Taylor" (her name for you, not mine). "Do *you* think I am making a mistake?" I told her she must make her own mistakes in her own way. She said: "I would never ask *you* or Elizabeth Bowen to alter a comma, but Liz Taylor's only a baby."' (This amused her very much.)

All this time, she was staring at my legs, and suddenly asked: 'Are those nylons you are wearing, or are you wearing no stockings at all?' I said they were the last pair of my nylons, memorial to my relationship with Blanche. 'Oh, she didn't ever give me nylons. I daresay she thought I was too frumpish.'

Blanche had summoned her to Claridge's to make impossible suggestions about 'The Present and the Past'. Either she didn't want to publish it this year, or not at all, but wanted her not to go to another publisher all the same. 'I could not understand what she said, because it was too preposterous *for* her to say.' She has followed my example (which she kindly applauded) and gone to another publisher.

She remembers her reviews and quotes them, knowing long passages by heart.

Your new book[4] was on the table by her chair and she said she had liked it very much – 'a good writer, a good interesting writer'. She repeated this four times, as she does.

Before I left, I asked if she would come to see me one day. She looked suspiciously and said how far, how long etc. Went into details of the journey, and then said: 'Well, then, perhaps I may.'

I hope I have remembered the things she said. I am writing almost at once, in case I forget. She only mentioned Margaret twice – once tenderly: 'the beautiful curtains Margaret and I chose together' – once tartly: 'Margaret would never prepare her lectures . . . just gather a few notes together and wonder why she was nervous at the last moment. In the end, I urged her not to do it.'

---

[4] *Some Principles of Fiction.*

It seems a grim, uncosy life there, but it appeared (yesterday at least) not to be having that effect upon her. She is thinking of her new novel ('Letting it germinate for a period') and seems very busy and hungry. She was not quite as neat as she used to be. Hair, the same grey tea-cosy streaked with gold. The same diamond ear-rings. The same interest in money. Knowing the price of everything. That intense love of flowers – a window-box with flox and fuchsias. 'People say the earth must be sour, but it has been there for eighteen years and still grows plants. What *is* sour earth?'

I was not quite sure, though confessed to having used the expression.[5] 'Then very honest of you to say so.' 'I love,' she said, 'to see a seed push out of the earth and crack in two. I should not want too many flowers.'. . . She asked why Blanche did not like my book[6] and kindly suggested that perhaps it was the woman being scarred from a motor accident which she didn't like (it was the book itself). 'But a very real modern problem it is, as being injured in war is too.' She said that with energy and emphasis and I was astonished ('when war casts its shadow I find that I recoil etc.').[7] She kept her eyes lowered to make sure that she did not look at me at this moment, at my own quite irrelevant scars. I kept my hands clasped tightly to avoid the habitual gesture of hiding myself from sight. The room froze with our self-control. I wished I could say: 'This is nothing to do with my book. Definitely not.' I so dreadfully wanted her to know that, although I am sure it is not really important either way. I think she felt awkward, because she quickly helped me to more raspberry-fool. Her hand shook and she spilt a lot into my glass.

'The raspberry fool and the dabs of cream is really literature,' I

[5] Tom uses the word (*Palladian*, p. 74); but he probably would not have known what it meant.
[6] *The Sleeping Beauty.*
[7] *A Conversation* (with Margaret Jourdain).

wrote back, '"the objective correlative". (I did not know you had scars, and I am glad I did not until now. I know they don't belong to your book – how beautifully you and She must have behaved. And how inevitably people argue falsely from any experience that an author has shared with a character: nearly always it meant something different. She would know that well enough). . . . I suppose Blanche Knopf calls her "Vy Burnett"?'

Elizabeth had sent me the hideous paper cover of the Italian translation of *A Wreath of Roses*, in shame marking it BURN. It represented the station scene at the beginning of the story.

The smartness of Camilla's luggage astonished me [I wrote] – and how modest not to write up UOMINI over what, I am sure, is the Gents. I tore it up, being unable to follow your instructions and burn it. I believe lots of things people want destroyed survive because they will say 'burn' dramatically, instead of 'destroy'. When I was in the Bodleian I was shocked at the existence of hundreds of letters the writers had marked 'burn'.

Elizabeth replied that one said 'burn' because fire is the only means by which writing can certainly be destroyed. Letters of her own to a friend had been pulled out of a waste-paper basket by the friend's husband, who did a jigsaw puzzle of the bits to find if there were signs that his wife had complained of him.

Rose Macaulay, so often mentioned by Ivy, was the only other person whom I have ever tried to meet – unsuccessfully, for dates did not fit. I could never quite get a picture of her from Elizabeth. 'In Cyprus I missed Rose Macaulay,' I told her,

whom I don't know, but think I should like, should I? Even though she quarrelled with your husband about motor cars. She hired one in Kyrenia and drove about recklessly – and very odd people were referring to her as 'Rosie' when I got there. A dreadful tragic place – elderly rheumatics dressing for dinner

at the hotel; artists not good enough; beach-combers not young
enough nor well enough off. It filled me with pity and terror.
Angus Wilson could write a cruel novel about Kyrenia. There is
a sort of club called 'Natter and Noggin' where the artists
exhibit pictures, and you can get cathedral tea-room sort of
food.

Elizabeth said that (like myself) she could never bring herself to
utter the words 'Natter and Noggin'; and she never had any need
to do so, for that establishment was no longer in existence when
she visited Kyrenia eighteen years later – and she rather liked the
place.

From Istanbul I went to Athens, and stayed there, never going
back to Cairo, where life had become increasingly difficult. Like
all British officials of the Egyptian Government I had been
dismissed from my university post eighteen months before, and I
was glad that the British Council was able to offer me a small post
in Athens, instead of piecework in Cairo. 'Nearer,' said Elizabeth,
but I think letters took quite as long. As she more than once said,
our letters over the years seemed to reveal a shockingly high
mortality among our friends. Apart from normal deaths, each of us
had to deplore the loss of two friends by suicide – one of these had
an almost traumatic effect upon her, I think. And a friend and
neighbour of hers, who played for the local cricket team, was
wantonly murdered by the poor, dreadful Ruth Ellis, the last
woman to be hanged in England.

In spring 1955 Gollancz published my book on Ivy's novels. As
the 'five chapters' Elizabeth and Ivy had already seen it, and after
one or two criticisms it had Ivy's imprimatur. She had thanked me
for 'the deep and exhaustive treatment', and added character-
istically: 'I cannot help being pleased – grateful though I should be
and am to her *in a way* – for Pamela Handford [sic] Johnson's
errors to be pointed out. She works in such haste that her words
cease to have a meaning, and a mind seems to be going to waste.
Ought the criticism of her to be a thought subdued before the book

comes out? Or may it stand as it is, and ought to be?' The conclusion seemed final to Elizabeth as to me, and the words stood. The book was, naturally, dedicated to Elizabeth, though I heard echoes of murmurings from London lady novelists. Ivy must have seen this to be right.

It was unfortunate that it should come out together with Ivy's least good novel. 'I want you to console me for what is inconsolable,' I wrote to Elizabeth.

> . . . What I mean is *Mother and Son.* . . . It is prosy and muddled: Plautus is wonderful (as good a cat as your horrible dog is as a dog), and there are excellent aphorisms. But . . . how can anyone think it her masterpiece! It is a great misfortune for my book to come out with it (though I am glad it was written before it): if it had only appeared with *The Present and the Past.* This goes far to explain the wretched press I have had – unfair both to her and me.

To Elizabeth also this book seemed disastrous – middlebrow, and Ivy imitating herself. We were immensely relieved to find, in her next book, that her powers were still unimpaired.

My friend (then, as British Council Representative in Greece, also my boss) Roger Hinks was delighted with Plautus, and was much intrigued by the phrase 'This is excellently made. . . . I regard cooking on this level as an accomplishment.' We used to speculate what the dish could have been. He wanted it to be an apple charlotte, but I did not want another in fiction after that in *Howards End.* Later, at what he called a 'Braemar gathering', he asked Ivy, but she did not seem to have anything particular in mind. I suspect it was a white cream, flavoured with rum.

Roger, an art historian, had first gone to the Mansions as Margaret's friend, and maintained that she had said: 'Of course I never read Ivy's trash.' He wrote to me some time later about a meeting with Ivy at Madge Ashton's when there was some talk about Angus Wilson.

Madge said: 'I hear he wrote it [*Anglo-Saxon Attitudes*] in four months, between 2 and 4 in the afternoon.' 'Really?' observed Ivy; 'one cannot imagine anyone doing anything in the afternoon between 2 and 4, except hoping that tea would be at 4 rather than at 5.' There was talk about how many words people wrote an hour. 'How many do you write, Miss Compton-Burnett?' said someone. 'Ten,' said Ivy, in the tone of an editor saying that this correspondence was now closed.

The following letter, written later in 1955, seems to be severely restricted to my eyes, but I think this restriction was lifted when, after Ivy's death, the letters were sent to Mrs Spurling:

I would not like to think of myself as a little Boswelly person, and my mother brought me up so much better than I have turned out. To abuse hospitality was the most horrid thing; worst of all. I often think how she would despise me when I am driven by curiosity to ask the children what they had for lunch when they were invited out. Loving does not cancel out such bad manners or excuse them, and she would not think so either. . . . The 'Mansions' seemed darker and more dreary than ever. I hate that black velvet on the chairs and sofa. A new maid. Four beautiful chairs had been recovered. '£2 a yard, but only two yards for the four' – a good sign, like the curtains. I was alone with her. She always seems shorter and plumper than I remembered. Sherry in a mauve glass. In the dining-room an electric fire each. Before mine, a half bottle of Graves toasting away. 'I think I'll move it now. I believe it shouldn't be *too* warm, I shall leave you to open it. Ernest Thesiger gave me that silly corkscrew and I don't know how to use it. He was very impertinent about my wine and said it always had pieces of cork floating in it. I am not very wine-wise, you know.' It is exactly the sort of corkscrew I always use but the room was so dark and I so flurried that I drove it in sideways and broke the cork. 'Well done!' she cried. It was indeed warm. Then she asked me if I

would have ice in it. She took hers 'on the rocks' as I believe
they say in America and then filled up with water and I realized
it was only broached for me. Before this there was a very deep
plate of vegetable soup. I was lapping away like mad. . . . Then
ham (she carves rather well. I was always surprised in the old
days that Margaret didn't carve), and a large potato in its
jacket. I excused myself but was ticked off for trying to slim.
'Potatoes are all water. You would have to eat six or eight of
these to put on weight.' The sweet warm wine, and too much
food. She asked if I had heard from you and said that she wished
to read the novel you were writing, and I'm afraid I said I
thought you were writing it. I'm sorry if I shouldn't. She said
this was excellent. 'He was very cut up about Stephen[8] dying,
They were so happy together. We went to tea with them in
Oxford. . . . I think they looked forward to going back there. It
never really works being an expatriate. I know several women
who have gone to live in Italy. They seem to settle down and
learn the language and then they suddenly become desperate
and want a crumpet or something.' We had a very white
pudding flavoured with rum ('I think she does this well'). She
told me that her other maid went mad in the spring. Poor Ivy
alone in the house with her and sudden strange conversations
about spiritualism and the stars. She had to be taken to hospital
and has since recovered. But Ivy found a 'very strange library'
in her room. 'So very peculiar. I didn't know that kind of thing
existed, but I have since learnt that there is quite a demand for
them. Horribly unpleasant. Quite a shock to me.' I hope I didn't
look too anticipatory, or too disappointed when she said they
were all about horoscopes and 'Find yourself through the Stars
etc', 'A very unhealthy lot.' When she recovered, I advised her
to get rid of them, and so she did. It was distressing to hear her
talking like that. When people are upset, I always say I have a
headache and that takes their mind off their troubles. But she

[8] The name given to my brother in my novels, and chosen by himself.

only said: 'I *knew* you had. I always know about you, because we are born under the same star.' 'That is carrying the democratic principle too far,' I said in a careless laughing way. 'What star is that?' 'I am afraid I don't remember,' she said coldly. (I was really asking for *you*). I kept asking silly questions and, trying to get a picture of the poor demented maid, asked how old she was. 'She was fifty-seven. It was nothing to do with the Change. That was years earlier.' Then: 'Be careful to wash those grapes thoroughly. They spray things over them. Won't you have a piece of fudge? I think you are rather a vain girl and thinking too much about your figure.' In the drawing-room was Olivia Manning's book. . . . 'It really is full of *very* good descriptions. Quite excellent descriptions. I don't know if you care for descriptions. I don't.' A little later, she glanced again at the book and said: 'A side of life I know nothing about. And I can't think how she does either.' She gave me a little frank talk about life in the trenches during the 1914 War and then suddenly asked: 'What about that murder? I saw the young man lived in Penn. . . .'

'Such dreadful things happen in families nowadays,' she said (I liked 'nowadays'). She couldn't find her handkerchief and said what a nuisance it is not to have pockets in frocks. 'I always stuff mine in the elastic of my breeks.' And indeed she does. For the rest, we disposed of Kingsley Amis (vulgar, dull and squalid) and Christianity ('not a good religion'). 'I don't find it charming when nuns behave so childishly. I know they are encouraged to, but it isn't pleasant to see middle-aged women clapping their hands and being excited and saying ridiculous things like: "Look at that pretty pink cushion!" It's all a pose. And as for monks in those silent orders they must be in a state of hysteria all the time. And quite sane friends of mine, whose opinions I respect over other things, believe in this terrible religion. Well, it is something I can't understand, and Rose Macaulay can't either.[9]

[9] Ivy cannot then have known that for some years Rose Macaulay had been a devout Anglo-Catholic.

I was brought up perfectly ordinarily in the Church of England but when I was sixteen or seventeen my reason naturally rejected such nonsense. No good can come of it. Its foundations are laid in fostering guilt in people – well, that obviously makes it easier for our Pastors and Masters when we are young. Margaret saw this when she was a little girl. She said to her governess: "I don't want to hear any more about that poor man," and walked out of the room.' She was full of vigour and indignation and those rather pretty diamond ear-rings swung to and fro. She is just beginning a new book – but 'work is the worst thing in the world'. 'I hear that anyone who rings up Elizabeth Bowen in the morning gets a pretty sharp retort. You would think she would be glad to be interrupted.' And then there were a lot of questions about money.

7

It was in the spring of 1956 that Elizabeth came to Greece for the first time, on a cruise. She did not then wish us to meet and I am glad that she did not – for us in Greece it was a painful time because of Cyprus, and I should not have wished to keep this from her, or to be speaking of it. But she had my *Aegean Greece*, which I hope said to her more what I should have wished to say.

> I think of you wherever I go [she wrote], all made lovelier by what you have written, in books or letters. Sometimes I feel frightened and sometimes tired from walking on a knife's edge, and also from seeing too many beautiful things. I loved the rooms full of those white anemones at Phaestos. That alone would have lasted a week and been enough to take in and remember.
>
> In a café in Rhodes three Englishwomen walked in wearing the most outlandish holiday clothes and panama hats, with lots of raincoats and cameras and walking-sticks and rucksacks. They stood looking about for a waiter and one said in a loud voice: 'How do we attract attention?'
>
> At Naxos it poured with rain and torrents swirled down those narrow streets. A lovely girl ran out of a house with an umbrella and held it over my head. It was a lucky thing, for she spoke French and I spent the rest of the day with her and her two friends, Lena and Maria. Very lovely girls. They took me all

over the Ursuline convent . . . and to meet the Reverend Mother – an old Irishwoman. The dormitories so clean and bare. When the rain stopped, we went up and walked on the roofs. There was a little wistfulness about these village girls when they looked at the rich convent girls in their expensive clothes. There was also wistfulness about Paros and whether I found it more beautiful, which I said I didn't – may I be forgiven. This made them wish to take me to see something more lovely on the island. In the end, we took a taxi and all went up to the mountainous part – a good way into the interior – to a little village called something like Kaloxilos, where Maria's grandmother lived and had a garden. The sun came out and the garden was dazzling and dripping wet. They loaded me with branches of lemons and bunches of stocks and carnations – overpoweringly sweet. The grandmother was a lovely old woman. She brought a tray of preserved oranges and then glasses of araki (?). When I left she picked up my scarf and tied it over my head. I loved those girls and was sad to leave them and know I would never see them again. One of them gave me a basket she had made and when I lifted the lid there was a card with her name in Greek and English, and the words 'For You'. . . .

But it was not all sweet at Naxos. It was not at all sweet for Alfred Noyes I learned when I came back to the boat, for he had a bucket of slops emptied on his head.

'The last man to take a thing like that well,' E.M. Forster said to Elizabeth – for he also was on that cruise and later they ate their hard-boiled eggs together, sitting high up in the theatre at Delphi, 'on the prompt side'. 'Salt is essential with eggs, I think,' Forster observed.

Elizabeth reacted to Greece as one would have been sure that she would – her love of flowers, of landscape and of the sea could still then be satisfied. In 1956 we still breathed pure air, even in Athens; the magic beauty of the countryside had not yet vanished from the most famous sites, and there was no discothèque on the islands. One would like to think that she even found it an advantage to be an ASROG, and that Miss B. and Miss T., who could take it in their stride, had prepared her to enjoy it. She could view with contempt those of her fellow tourists who, after the Aegean, could excite themselves over the meretricious charms of Venice.

About this time I wrote to her:

And now Joyce Cary is here, do you know him? . . . She [Ivy] said to him: 'Mr Cary, there comes a moment when my book sets, like that jam in that jar.'

I dined with Roger [Hinks] when Joyce Cary failed to turn up – his aeroplane crashed and, soaked in kerosene I believe, he gallantly leapt into the next. He was to come in the small hours, so Roger had to leave a note for him.

'Is there any well-known author you don't know already with whom you'd *like* to spend all the time I have to spend with him?' asked Roger plaintively.

'I don't think so – Claudel would be unthinkable.'

'I'd want to club him on the head with a *soulier de satin* after two hours,' said Roger, in a harsh hurrying tone. 'Well, now I must write *L'annonce faite à Cary.*'

Another long Braemar letter dates from early 1957.

I should be correcting proofs,[1] but my eyes hurt. Since Tuesday, when I went to tea with Ivy, I have been living in a dream of confusion and discomfort. It was a dreadful occasion. I was determined to get to the Whitechapel Road to see the George Stubbs Exhibition and *not* to take a taxi. I felt a sense of achievement, but vertigo too, and sat on a great red dais in the middle of the gallery and tried to keep my eyes open. So

[1] These must have been those of *Angel* (1957).

Braemar Mansions was a sad ending. I was utterly depressed
and silences fell in which she steadfastly looked away and then
took a quick little bite of a glance. I had arranged myself (while
she arranged the flowers I'd brought) with my back nearly to
the light. But 'you will be more comfortable *here*,' she said, and I
meekly sat opposite those long dusty windows. (I know that
parapet across the road by heart.) I could not argue or explain,
or feel anything but fatigue and dismay. She gave me a piece of
bread and a toasting fork and we both crouched over the fire to
make toast. Everything domestic I do very quickly. 'Are you
sure you've done both sides? I don't think you can have in the
time.' She was in a very whispering, repeating mood. 'That's
right,' she kept saying to herself. I was glad you had warned me
about the Rent Restriction Act, because it began as soon as I
arrived. 'I suppose you *bought* your new house?' 'Yes.' 'I suppose
you paid a high price.' 'Yes.' 'How much?' hung in the air. I
wanted her to ask it, but she wouldn't so it didn't emerge. I so
much wanted her to ask that I wouldn't tell her.

It seemed so awful to me there, shabby in a cold and desolate
way and so dusty and all of the sofa taken up by stacks of
cushions arranged like books on a bookshelf. So many
unreflecting looking-glasses, three big ones hanging in a row
above the fireplace, but too high for anyone to look into.

Flaky pastry from my Banbury cake cascaded on to my knees.
'Perhaps you don't usually eat tea. I have only a very light meal
in the middle of the day. T.S. Eliot told me that if he misses his
tea he is no good for anything until he has had it the following
day.' (Silly old woman, I thought, making such a fuss.) She
talked a great deal about T.S. Eliot – his rent restriction fears
and his new wife. 'She is tall and fair and fair-skinned, a nice
green dress, good-looking I should say, although it was artificial
light and I should think she looks very different in the day time
. . . yes, I should think *very* different. Apparently she's always
adored him, although she was his secretary for years. I am sure
that if I had been his secretary for a fortnight I should have

wanted to poison him, not marry him . . . yes, I should have run round to the chemist's for threepennyworth of poison after a very short time. John Hayward, with whom he used to live, is keeping on the old flat, and Eliot has paid up the rent for another two years. There was a good deal of talk about that . . . no, I don't think there really was much talk. I think I just asked a lot of impertinent questions. People say that if you don't ask you get told more, but I have never found that to be true. I have found that one gets told nothing at all. Yes, I expect you did have to give a lot for your house. People do. . . .'

I feel nervous, too, about the new short BBC novel.[2] She has to have the money, though, because goodness knows what her rent will be, and Rose Macaulay says *she* will not pay a penny more but Rose will do exactly what everyone will have to do and pay what she is told. Ah, naughty headstrong Rose.

The question of Miss Ironside was brought up, but not by me. 'A very handsome woman with a dark skin, West Indian blood, I suspect. She asked me to a cocktail-party to which I didn't want to go, so I said I had a cold which wasn't true at the time but knowing my chest I guessed that I should have a bronchial cough at any moment and so I did. And then I thought I would write and suggest that she should suggest herself to tea one day and not only did she have the effrontery to do so but she brought her husband. As soon as Rose knew that she was coming, she said that she must come too, and challenge her statements about Margaret's sister. For so much was untrue, and Margaret never doubted her sister's integrity; they really believed, poor things, that what they said was true, and Miss Ironside or whatever her name is seems to have had some grudge against her. Then everybody wanted to come to tea. They swarmed in and I had to have a cup that didn't match the saucer. Lots of people had to be refused. I couldn't just have them standing at the back. It became out-of-hand and I had to stop Rose, for after all Miss

[2] This novel, read on the wireless before publication, was *A Father and His Fate*.

Ironside was my guest and she was getting very angry and upset. I believe she has written other books, you know, though I am sure I don't know what they are. . . .'

Before I left, she gave me a long talk on the re-wiring of her flat and asked if *we* have old-fashioned fuse-boxes. 'None at all,' I said. 'You must have *some*. They just haven't come to your notice.' I don't know why, but it seemed important to me to establish that we haven't any fuse-boxes (and indeed we haven't), but she wouldn't allow this and was quite stern with me about it as if I were deliberately lying to her. 'It takes, they say, seven years to make an electrician; and I did it in a fortnight.' By this time she had decided that I was utterly irresponsible (in spite of my record toast-making), and she said that I should wear warmer clothes. 'Or you'll be laid up. If you are, I hope you'll do as I did and be careful with yourself and don't be tempted to take risks. It is quite all right for you to get up and go along to the bathroom, but you should put on your stockings *and* your knickers. A loose night-gown and a dressing-gown is no proof against draughts.'

This letter calls for further comment. It was an odd thing that T.S. Eliot and Ivy, our two greatest writers at that time, should live near to each other, and near St Stephen's, Gloucester Road, where he worshipped and she did not. One would like to detect a mutual influence. The plot of *The Family Reunion* is reminiscent of some of her novels, and the reference to 'Compton-Smith's place in Dorset' could be an acknowledgement and a private joke – though Mr Smith of Compton occurs in *Mansfield Park*. And the rhythm of her dialogue in some of the later books at times recalls his free hexameters.

The three looking-glasses were among the fifteen bequeathed by Ivy to literary friends. It has been suggested that she had a secret, ironic intention, but I doubt it: she wished to give souvenirs to a number of people, and that there should be no cause for jealousy between them – though I am told that jealousy arose.

Elizabeth did not get one, and that may have been a tribute to her good taste; she would have had no room in her house for such an object. Perhaps it was also a tribute to her good looks (if Ivy were really being naughty): Elizabeth need not have feared to face it.

'Miss Ironside' was Lucille Iremonger, author of *The Ghosts of Versailles*, in which the 'vision' of *An Adventure* is attacked as an imposture, and Eleanor Jourdain is treated with scant respect. This is not surprising in view of Eleanor Jourdain's extraordinary conduct some years later when, as Principal of St Hugh's College, she accepted the resignation of the entire staff. Even with regard to this episode Margaret showed a sisterly loyalty: I am told that when she and Ivy found themselves staying at the same hotel as Cecilia Ady, Eleanor Jourdain's chief opponent, 'there was a marked coldness'.

Of course John, her husband, told Elizabeth that Ivy had been right about the fuse-boxes: they just hadn't come to her notice, so she had to eat humble pie. In my ignorance of electricity I would have believed her, even if it sounded unusual.

'It was a little alarming', I wrote, 'to think there was anyone so far above human weakness as to have none. And of course it is the sort of thing one would have told people – something special, idiosyncratic and yet not too intimate about you, and a trait in which (naturally) you seemed to take some pride. . . .'

Ivy had gone on to ask about me: '"I believe he is in rather low spirits. Do you know what *sort* of low spirits? But I expect it is the effects of expatriation. Always a mistake. I hear he's given up his lecturing. But he has private means, you know." Perhaps a reticent look came upon my face, for she didn't pause after her questions or seem expectant of any replies.'

But I had not voluntarily given up my 'lecturing'; my institute had closed on account of the Cyprus situation, and I had to make do with inadequate 'private means', even 'touching capital', which would have deeply shocked Ivy. So far from craving for crumpets I was firmly resisting repatriation and trying hard to stay where I was; the kindness of friends enabled me to do so. Nevertheless, there was cause for lowness of spirits. Cyprus (to use a favourite expression of Elizabeth's) was taking its toll of her too, for Renny, her son, was doing his military service there. 'I have a brother, but he's away from home at present,' wrote Joanna tactfully to a Greek pen-friend.

Angel appeared in this year. Mark Ogilvie-Grant, another Athenian pen-friend and later a friend of hers, echoed my thoughts when he said: '. . . a good book, but she didn't write it'. Some time before he had asked me if I knew this most neglected of novelists, coming up to talk to me in a blue-green Athenian bar from which he was almost at once to be evicted for a splendid falsetto rendering of 'The Lost Chord'. 'Indistinguishable', he said, 'from Clara Butt at her prime.'

At the time I conjectured – and she said doubtfully that I might be right – that she was thus exorcizing the spirit of 'ferocity, brutality, violence', which had tempted her artist in *A Wreath of Roses* away from her true world, and made her fearful of being 'ladylike, nostalgic, governessy'. But it is far from these things. It is the story of a violent, self-hypnotized novelist of the Ouida class: a writer as different from Elizabeth as one can imagine. It is larger than her earlier work, but more nearly anonymous, not so marked with the idiosyncratic personality which so much delights readers in most of her novels and stories. Angel herself is not wholly in context, and at times the author's attention slipped. In a household that has adopted vegetarianism a leg of mutton makes an unexplained appearance; and it is very much there, for Angel and her companion quarrel about the lack of red-currant jelly.

Cautiously, I asked her about this. She wrote:

I almost fainted when I read your letter, confronted by that terrible mistake I had made. The kind I make continually, but had hoped not to make in my work. One side of my mind seems to slip. If only you had read it first – as at least six people did without realising. If I could do that I could do anything, as a chef once said to me when I told him he had sprinkled sugar on a

steak and kidney pie. It must be, for my peace of mind, another
of those places on which I lock a door and turn my back.

This morning there was a letter from Ivy. 'You have served
your theme well, and to my mind it is one that both needed and
deserved the service.' I should love to read a reference by her
for a maid leaving her employment. . . . She finishes – 'I hope
that "Angel" is having the kind of attention it merits. The other
kind does not matter.'

From time to time, between the novels, Elizabeth's stories
began to appear. They did not express or reveal but played with
her own experience, or she wove fancies from tiny fragments of
fact – at least this I sometimes thought I recognized. Like Henry
James, she found the tiny 'germ' in a happening, and then had to
create people to bring it about; unlike Turgenev, who began with
creating people, and then watched and listened for what they
would do or say. But her happenings were transformed by the
characters who caused or suffered them; she was an artist, unlike
the Goncourts, who attached happenings to characters quite
arbitrarily to suit their convenience.

The story 'You'll Enjoy It when You Get There' is an amusing
expansion of a gaffe of her own at a 'trade banquet'; but the central
figure is a young girl deputizing for her mother. 'Poor Girl' has a
little of her life as a governess: her brilliant pupil is there, but not
his parents. This was written for Lady Cynthia Asquith's ghost
book. Lady Cynthia (like Elizabeth) had lately been to Haworth
and was delighted with it: 'I shall write a new book about the
Brontës, *Three Lucky Girls*,' she remarked.

The story that most nearly touched me was 'The Letter-
Writers'. It was not, as Elizabeth said, about herself and me – and
yet there was something in it of our predicament, that of two
correspondents who have never met. Her Edmund (who lives in
Rome) is more distinguished than I could ever be, and she was
never so humble as her Emily. But they have written to one
another for ten years, hardly knowing why, and perhaps have

found the greater satisfaction in it because it is a luxury, not the fulfilment of a need. 'As she wrote, the landscape, flowers, children, cats and dogs, sprang to life memorably.' While Edmund, who does not care to live in England 'from old vexatious associations' likes none the less 'to have some foothold there'.

After ten years' correspondence they venture to meet. The circumstances are outwardly disastrous. Edmund arrives to find Emily's cat has got at the lobsters and broken her beautiful china; and in a moment of quiet at the end of his visit a boring neighbour (well known to him from the letters) makes her way in – and alas, like most bores who are funny in letters, she is not so in real life. It would seem that everything between them has been ruined – but no, they decide to treat the day as if it had never been; and when he has gone Emily picks up her goose-quill pen and again writes 'Dear Edmund'.

After that story I dare say she felt that we could meet – for though it had not been 'taken from the life' it had, as Elizabeth's very solid stories were apt to do, taken on life. It had happened – and nothing worse was likely to happen – and it had done no harm.

8

At first she was undecided. 'I am not very good at travelling on my own. I am always punctual and on the platform in plenty of time, but it is seldom the right platform. If I stayed in Athens I could go to places from there, I thought. And I should feel better having the knowledge that you were nearby if I suddenly became unhinged.' She had just been shaken by a 'terrible adventure'.

I let myself be persuaded to take part in a television programme about books. I sat on one of those contemporary chairs with spindly legs and talked to a poor woman who had got me as a prize for writing something about *A Wreath of Roses*. For this escapade we had to go to Birmingham for the weekend. Angus Wilson, entering the station hotel, said 'Everything exactly as in "You'll enjoy it when you get there".' The trouble was there was no chance of that. My Mrs Hewitt from the Lake District was so nice and I felt she was an old friend, but we wanted to talk about our Christmas shopping, not books. And the lights were so bright that I could hardly bear it and my eyes are still burning. It was all a great mistake. It is difficult to believe that a writer who writes such drivel as does Paul Gallico could be so unpleasantly deluded with grandeur. Angel wasn't in it. There was a sinister and often rehearsed entrance wearing a long cloak and looking like Count Dracula. 'Mr *Wilson's* kind, but *he* makes me feel out of it,' whispered Mrs H. Mr Wilson was indeed kind. I could not have got through it without him. He is funny too. I liked him so very much. He – in his little bit, sitting on a different spindly chair – had the presence of mind to take the opportunity of delivering an onslaught on the Snow school of criticism, the stranglehold they have, their implication that there are worthwhile characters who 'matter' and others that cannot have any importance. 'I don't give a damn for what is fashionable,' he said, 'and I don't want to write about characters just because they're fashionable types. Not even scientists or Cambridge dons. . . .' Next time the Snows are on the programme: 'It would be nice if you and I could take them on and split them up,' Mr Wilson said. 'I don't think we should win but everyone would think we were nicer people.'

Elizabeth had particularly suffered from the Snowbound school of reviewers; being insensitive to the charm of her work, they found it trivial. They objected that her people did not act, but merely behaved. As I wrote in an article on her:[1]

This objection may be made about most human beings as well as about most fictional characters at the present time, when there is no accepted common standard. A Christian writer, like Rose Macaulay,[2] had a standard for her people; Miss Compton-Burnett, an intensely moral writer, has the standards of late nineteenth century, upright, liberal and enlightened agnosticism, personally modified but firmly held. Some recent writers have tried to apply standards that are social rather than ethical, with the consequence that they have been very boring, and have made mistakes about individuals. Others, notably Mr Forster, have tried to elevate a personal aesthetic or mystique into a moral theory, and often it has wobbled over into sentimentality. It is a great merit in Mrs Taylor that she has been content to be

---

[1] *A Review of English Literature*, 1, no. 2 (1960).
[2] For so she always was, *pace* Ivy.

guided by her moral taste, which is very fine and true, without trying to form a set of principles upon it.

Her people when they are important are moral agents; and when they are good they are usually nice as well. Moreover they are interesting; it is to the reader that characters have to matter, and they will not unless they interest him.

'Mrs Taylor does not seem to me to be very like Mrs Woolf or Miss Compton-Burnett or Miss Bowen,' I had written, for some reviewers thought her too heavily indebted to them.

Her feet seem to me to be set more firmly upon the earth than theirs. . . . Let us take a homely example. I have heard it objected that in every book of hers there is a smell of onions, and that this is intended to show observation. I thought all the world smelt of onions; I should expect a writer to choose a less ubiquitous smell to show observation. And it is not true . . . that every one of Mrs Taylor's books smells of them. Mrs Woolf must, indeed, have used onions in the famous *boeuf en daube*, but neither she nor Miss Bowen nor Miss Compton-Burnett ever admits to having smelt one – though in her different way each of them conveys that the whole of domestic life (of which onions are a part) is her province.

Elizabeth wrote, acknowledging a draft of this article: 'I am grateful for what you wrote. It is puzzling when people say I write like this one and that one and all such different *kinds* of writers and so many of them, and it makes me feel I am nothing in myself.' But she insisted that Elizabeth Bowen was also down to earth:

Untidy kitchens with smells – not babies, because I'm sure she dislikes them, but marriage and women's friendships – I think she can do this in an everyday *true* way. I think my babies and animals are good and I enjoy doing it. . . . I'm awfully glad you think I can be funny. It is not much remarked on. A sense of the incongruity of things is not so unimportant as some people think. Even if it's not used, it's a good piece of equipment to have and would help some serious writers – Iris Murdoch, for one – not to fall into dreadful traps of bathos and sententiousness. Of course, the Snows couldn't be funny if they tried.

Her happy hunting-ground for the grotesque was among the 'non-U', and in this I think her researches anticipated those of Nancy Mitford and Professor Ross. She did a good deal of field-work in the pubs of commuterland, achieving in her story 'Summer Schools' (also in the 1958 volume) an almost 'Gothic' horror. Its characters live their absurd lives in a décor that might have been invented by Osbert Lancaster or Sir John Betjeman at their best. This is the world explored by one of her two schoolmistresses. In comparison, the other visits a world, a boys' preparatory school in a Georgian house full of earnest people listening to lectures on 'the novel', that might be thought almost civilized. Better the weary smell of minced beef and boiled cabbage than the acrid stench of Virginian cigarettes, the mawkish smell of warm beer, and whisky and petrol fumes. Better the mild academic joke than the jollities of the saloon bar. Elizabeth reported that she had heard in such a place: 'Long time, no see, old boy, what's your poison?' 'I think you would have got up and walked out, but I wanted to stay on for ever.' She was indeed made of sterner stuff than myself. 'Now I shall pour myself a drink,' she wrote. '"Astonishing good health to you, Liz old girl," I shall say. "Long time no see."'

She had had a glimpse of the academic sort of 'summer school' when she went to Oxford to lecture on Ivy to some foreign students. But she found hardly anyone who wanted to talk to her afterwards apart from an American girl who admired her frock, and asked her to guess what they had had for luncheon. It was macaroni cheese and mashed potatoes.

Finally she decided to come to Greece again. 'Being on my own will be a relief. If I get lost, at least I shan't lose other people.'

She stayed at the Xenias Melathron, a little old hotel that has since been pulled down, but has an after-life in her story 'The Voices', to which the amusing waiter Polycarp, who brought her breakfast to her, also contributed.

She had asked if there were anything I wanted from England, and I asked her to bring a large, old-fashioned teddy bear for my small Greek godson, George. I said that if she would leave it with the bill at her hall-porter's desk, she could trust me to take it and leave the money without attempting to see her. She replied that of course she could trust me, but that this time she would like us to meet. I asked her to come to see me on the day after her arrival and at the hour of sunset, the best time for the wonderful view that I then had to offer her. I suggested by what way she could come. I knew that she would be feeling timid, and it was rather a climb in any case: comforting for her to come up a flight of steps passing a trellis of gloriously flowering wistaria.

A bell rang, and I pressed the button that opened the front door. 'Is that Elizabeth?'

'Yes,' said a timid voice.

I had moved a table into a big window, for I foresaw that we should need all the help we could get from the view. 'That is Salamis, that is Aegina. Far to the left you can see Hydra.'

Soon she began telling me of a tasteless fellow-passenger of hers who, at this time the day before, had kept his nose buried in *Doctor Zhivago* while they flew in exquisite weather over the Gulf of Corinth. Then I administered a little ouzo and we began to talk about Ivy. Finally I ventured to ask her to come and dine with me in the Pláka, which had not then become a pandemonium. By the end of the evening we were talking easily, like the old friends we were. The huge teddy bear had been installed on a chair in my flat, and scared my servant when she came in next morning.

There were several high points during her visit. One day we went for an excursion with my godson George and his young parents, George clutching teddy, nearly as big as himself. Elizabeth was always delightful with pleasantly smiling people who wanted to be pleasant – and it is reposeful when one does not have to talk or understand their language. In her unsentimental way she loved children, though no one was better aware of their knavish tricks. She and I agreed that what we really envied them for was the power of crying when they are bored or, as an extreme measure, being sick. We should dearly have loved to have cried or been sick on many a social occasion. She was enchanted with green and flowery Attica (as in spring it still is), and the little landlocked bay of Porto Ráfti that was then still 'real country'.

One day we had luncheon with her other Athenian fan, Mark Ogilvie-Grant, at his pretty house. 'You observe', he said, 'we are not having lobster.' He was a very judicious admirer of her work, often quoting minor felicities like the baby smelling of milk (*A Wreath of Roses*) or the cat (in 'Summer Schools') whose 'hunched-up body, blown feathery by the wind, gave him the look of a barn owl'. A woman present asked if Elizabeth were my sister, and at one time I wished she had been – but better not, for she would have lost an adored and incalculable mother and gained a dreadfully unhappy home; and it would be a pity if we had shared the same literary material. She, on her side, had always the sisterly feeling of wanting to 'thump' anyone who exploited me or tried to do me down.

When she went to stay for a day or two on Hydra, I accompanied her on the morning boat, and left her there. We had time for a short walk on a rocky path before I had to return to Athens. I remember that we agreed that for nothing on earth would we be young again. We were then both at a very comfortable period of life, and I don't know why no one has ever prayed to the gods for perpetual middle age. I am sure there were also 'pretty severe philippics' against some other authors and critics, especially the Snowbound school – though I have never (as far as I know) had any reason for personal animus against them.

When I left, my place was taken by a dog: 'He took me over completely, and came everywhere but to Church with me, and saw me back to the hotel at night. It was a nice, loose relationship, and I never saw him again.' She had gone to church to hear the Salutations of Our Lady, an office sung on Lenten Fridays and always well attended: an occasion to see the people of Hydra. A woman standing next to her thrust a baby into her arms, and with her usual politeness she stayed holding it long after she would have liked to go away.

On her last evening, after I had said goodbye to her, I happened to pass by a café in which she was sitting, pensively reading a newspaper. I knew better than to go in. Later she told me: 'I was keeping up my homework, studying form.' While in Athens she had got her hall-porter to place a successful bet for her on a horse called Beethoven, and I am sure she was acting on the best information that was to be had. She told me how sad it made her to go to races and see young people throwing their money away – had their parents never taught them to study form?

Six weeks or so later my novel *The Rivers of Babylon* came out. 'Ivy', I told Elizabeth, 'wrote me a very handsome letter, as handsome (I should think) as Mr Frank Churchill's to poor-Miss-Taylor-that-was. It began "My dear Robert", and ended "yours as ever". She said: "I never thought to enjoy a book about a foreign country so much" – she liked the expatriates, because they lived in the past. She also said, "The humour and tragedy and grace remain with me."'

While Elizabeth was in Athens I had given her a proof copy. I now quote her too kind words because they show some of the things she valued in writing, even if I imperfectly deserve such praise.

> You write quietly about overwhelming things, no fuss or fury, and never for half a sentence have you ever bored me. . . . I am moved by those cadences I find in Ivy. What is most true and touching is in a dying fall, said hardly at all, or in a low, quick way or turning aside. One's throat is caught. But you are also very funny and strippingly caustic and not too ruthful about what seems contemptible to you, or tiresome. I ran to your

reviews as if they were my own and felt more dismay and indignation than if they *had* been. Such fools they make of themselves. . . . When they say that nothing happens I wonder what they want to happen. It seemed to me that as much happened as I could bear. . . . And 'how much happens' isn't a valid point of criticism, anyhow. 'My father has come. He is in the hall at this moment', sends me into a panic not milder certainly than any I have ever felt in all the catastrophes of War and Peace. Pour cool scorn on them and forget. I have just been dreadfully belaboured in the London Magazine. I am still licking my wounds. It was so awful that my agent, unknown to me, wrote to protest and John Lehmann said he was very sorry because he, personally, held me in high regard. . . .

The insensitive reviewer had invented and made use of the horrible word 'Bowenoid' for the stories collected in *The Blush* – he found them penetrating and subtle but could not forgive Elizabeth for her good fortune in being able to please the simple as well as the highbrow reader. This is enviable good luck and financially profitable, and when it happens to a writer whose standards are not thereby lowered only prigs will think less of the work. There is a great deal of work in these stories, they are not slick. The reviewer grudgingly found amusement in the tale of a pub-crawling young bridegroom who strolled into the bar while his wife was donning the mauve chiffon nightgown that was to excite him. He met people, made friends and absent-mindedly let them drive him home to his parents, forgetting the bride upstairs who was waiting for him to come and claim his 'marital rights'. It is a funny story, but it seems that the reviewer mainly liked it because it was not very likely to please the editor of a women's magazine. But his unkindest cut at Elizabeth was to call her heartless; she had only too much heart for her comfort.

9

That summer of 1959 Elizabeth's son, Renny, was appallingly injured in a motor accident. It was Elizabeth's courage and devotion that kept him alive until his own courage could take over. This experience 'took its toll' of her. She told me that in the first dreadful night, when she and John stayed in the hospital, she had tried to soothe the time by the old paper game of making words out of words. Strange words she chose; on the back of a letter of mine I found words made out of HORSELESS and NOVELIZE.

Later in the year Ivy's novel *A Heritage and Its History* appeared. 'It has been Ivy week,' wrote Elizabeth.

The book emerged on Monday, on Wednesday was broadcast as a play, on Thursday Daniel George (Dan, Dan, the literary man, John calls him) spoke on the wireless and said she was the greatest writer of her day, and on Sunday morning the book was discussed by a querulous little bunch called 'The Critics', who seem to be part of the Establishment, and on Sunday afternoon, lo and behold, the television (commercial) went into Braemar Mansions itself, where she was interviewed by Alan Pryce-Jones [then Editor of *The Times Literary Supplement*]. . . . My heart was knocking wildly. The camera hovered in a sinister way over Cornwall Gardens, the grim outside. It looked like the beginning of a murder film. Then, once inside, I felt better. The high, light, pretty voice, the mouth pursed yet smiling. The eyes . . . sometimes looking bewildered, even desperate, but I think it was the horrible bright lights which are the worst part of it all. It was the same programme that I was in. . . . She was most amusing, and described how much she had been abused by reviewers and how one man wrote to her asking her to explain what on earth her books were all about, and enclosed a stamped and addressed envelope for her reply – 'I used it when I was paying a bill'. When asked which, was her favourite of her books, she said: 'Well, I do really rather like "Manservant and Maidservant".' 'I'm very fond of "A House and Its Head",' said Mr Pryce-Jones. 'Yes, I like that very much too,' she said enthusiastically. 'I rather like them all, in fact. After all, they are mine.' She was very firm about not liking cats. 'Is it a fact that you don't like any animals?' 'Oh, no, I like them in their proper places. I like cows in the field, and pigs in the pig-stye [sic] and hens in the hen-run. But I shouldn't like to have animals inside the house. . . .' 'Would you say that the production of a novel is something akin to the process of childbirth?' (My heart jumped into my mouth.) 'Of course I know nothing about the process of childbirth,' she said, with an austere expression about her lips. . . .

It's good, isn't it? In its own extremely pared down way. I like more richness – as in Manservant and Maidservant. It's much more Greek, and I see her smiling to herself when she wrote Walter's words – 'It was like a Greek tragedy. With people saying things with a meaning they did not know, or with more meaning than they knew.' I think she sometimes falls to the temptation of disarming critics. It sounded on the wireless like a very plain translation of a Greek play. Aloud, it seems more measured. I think it is more measured than the others, and I would rather it were not. I love Simon very much. He will go among my favourites. The book has a satisfying pattern and a unity one wouldn't expect in anything covering that span of years and when Simon, at the end, wanted to leave the creeper as it was, the wheel had turned full circle. Who cares whether

Walter went to Oxford or Cambridge?[1]

I feel more that it was her *father*. You know what I mean.[2] Mothers would never speak of workhouses. And someone has. I almost dare suggest myself again and take a stiff brandy and ask a lot of questions that we want to know the answers to. Stake everything. She would at once understand the motive and, however coldly she dealt with me, she would understand the necessity.

A little later:

I wrote to Ivy, and this is from her letter. 'I did not see the television, as even my friends who had it had not the Independent; and the only person who saw it seemed to be the greengrocer, who naturally had everything.

'There are rumours of a novel from you, I trust well-founded. I am waiting for it eagerly, as so few are to one's mind in these days. And those that are are met by reviewers with an odd undercurrent of grievance that is hard to explain. Or perhaps it is not.'

I am also bidden to suggest myself.

A little later:

Madge Garland had a terrible experience, which I can sympathize with. Rebecca West has often plainly hinted that I should arrange a meeting with Ivy, whom she dearly wished to see. 'She won't come to the country,' I said – pretending that it didn't occur to me that there were other ways. Madge Garland, however, fell for it and, although scared, invited them both to lunch. Rebecca was apparently at her most scintillating – brilliant talker as she has the reputation of being. She put everything into it, and Ivy simply lopped off everything she said

[1] By a slip, he appears to go to both.
[2] The original 'tyrant'.

and left it lying there, dead. Feverishly she went on and coldly
Ivy felled her. Gaps grew in the conversation – unimaginable in
Rebecca's presence. Silences fell and lengthened. Poor hostess!
She should have known how it would be. I should like to hear
Rebecca's version, but can only do so if I repair my rudeness and
invite them here – (Like the Queen, we never ask her back).

At the end of the year:

I have re-read *A House and its Heritage* [*sic*]. Simon is truly
wonderful, I think. He explains much of what went before. We
have never watched before how the tyranny began. I loved him
at the beginning and could not hate him later – even when he
was agonizing everyone. There is too Biblical a ring about the
language – especially in the brief bits of narrative. Julia is good,
and unlike anyone else. But Walter is a poor shade of what we
have had better done.

I was in a café in Beaconsfield waiting for a bus, and at the
next table a man and a woman were passionately discussing Ivy.
I had to turn and look at them. It was as much as I could do not to
join in. Of course she is becoming more well known and it is not
always easy to realise it.

Workhouses. One need not know about them to hold them out
as a threat. I was taken over one by my History mistress. There
were rows of beds, covered with scarlet blankets and on each
one at the pillow end was a large, white, upturned chamber pot.

'Ivy writes', I told Elizabeth at this time,

(thanking me for my congratulations on her beautiful master-
piece): 'It is hopeless the way life has to change, and become less
than life. It just has to be accepted. . . . This, I thought, rather
an excessively sympathetic comment – I had only said that I
was very sorry that Roger [Hinks] had been transferred.
Perhaps the Rent Act was behind it.

About the withheld novel of mine she wrote nobly: 'It must not be spoiled by being adapted to the sensibilities of living persons. It is better to hold it still. It may live beyond their lives and should not suffer from them.'

In another letter about this time, Elizabeth explained a reference to 'the dark room' at Braemar Mansions:

The dark room is the dining-room, with its view of the wall and the fire escape. 'We will go into the dark room in a minute,' she said. It is all so depressing. I haven't been into her bedroom though I saw some chair legs and a pair of shoes as I passed the half-open door. When I am departing she whispers 'Would you like to. . . ?' but I have always said 'no'. Once she was out of her chair I should not like to keep her hanging about, and I can always make straight for the Ladies at Harvey Nicholls [sic].

Elizabeth visited Ivy not long after the University of Leeds had given her an honorary doctorate, in May 1960.

I found a difference in Ivy after such a time. I'm afraid she looked much older and frailer. It was the first time I had seen her in a pale colour – a light grey dress which made her seem shadowy. Yet she eats so much. She put a great many potatoes on my plate after she had served the hot salmon. We had stewed morella [sic] cherries and a rum-flavoured thing in a very large glass dish (had been broached). It was a Port Salut that had gone through all its stages this time. She was in a gay and lively mood. I went into the kitchen as she asked me to have a few words with the 'factotum' ('She seems to be rather taken with your looks'). The factotum is new – a very Irish little thing – wearing a cap – 'as a concession'. 'She pretends she is a Nurse. How did you know she is Irish?' I was asked when I mentioned this. Of course I got nowhere and she found out all she cared to know about me (though not about my friends). We were talking about flowers and I mentioned the wild garlic which I had seen growing in Wiltshire. 'Such a pretty flower,' she said. 'I have seen it in Kent.' Boldly I mentioned what Kay Dick wrote about her. 'I wish she wouldn't,' she said crossly. 'It is so gossippy [sic]. After all, people don't want to know about *me*, but about my books.' She is very cross with Henry Green who had said in an interview in a French newspaper that she was a governess. She asked me about Mr Forster on the cruise and I told her about the salt. She was amused at first and then became grave and after a pause said: 'Of course, he's perfectly right.' She thinks he is not at all the great genius he is made out to be – just possesses a pleasing talent.

She asked me about your novel. 'It is all about his step-mother isn't it?' And then she made a noise that sounded like Ho-Hum. We talked about shopping a great deal. Although she grumbles that T.S. Eliot does so much, she is all game for it herself. She brings home everything except potatoes and anyone who says that one can't get fresh vegetables in London must do her shopping by telephone, she is convinced.

The thing about her D.Litt. was the expense. It was a very costly business – three pounds ten a day – not a week – to stay at the Queen's Hotel at Leeds. She went into the men's robing room by mistake when she put on her gown but no one seemed to mind. At the grand banquet she toasted herself in champagne owing to confusion. She had no idea how to proceed during the ceremony and was relieved that a man had to go first. She watched very carefully and did exactly as he did except that when he had given two low bows she did 'two quick bobs'.

It must be explained that Kay Dick had published an article in which she stated that Ivy descended from Bishop Burnet and a Compton heiress from Wiltshire: 'the place was sold', apparently in her grandfather's time, according to this account. But Kay has admitted (in her charming *Ivy and Stevie*) that she sometimes had difficulty in deciphering her notes, and that Ivy was often mysterious and contradictious. I think that, without convicting her of telling taradiddles to improve her genealogy, we may well suspect her of having allowed Kay to mislead herself.

Nor is it impossible that she believed this legend. Her father's biographer, Dr J.H. Clarke, mentioned the Bishop as an ancestor and added: 'The name Compton was taken about the year 1770, on the marriage of James's grandfather with a Miss Compton of Hampshire, a lady of large fortune, at whose desire the addition was made.' It is most unlikely that Ivy knew that this Miss Compton was a blacksmith's daughter, and her 'fortune' a loan of £300.

Elizabeth never much believed in the 'place', but she and John did some detective work in Wiltshire. Compton This and Compton That were explored in vain, even Compton Scorpion. But, wading through long grass and nettles in country churchyards, they found nothing. I had imagined a battered tomb of Dame Alyse Compton, or a fine eighteenth-century tablet sacred to the memory of William Compton-Burnett and Hepzibah his wife, and lodge gates surmounted by heraldic monsters bearing the achievements of (quarterly 1 and 4) Burnett, and Compton (2 and 3).

Bishop Burnet I gave up with even more regret than the 'place.' A daughter of his was the mother of Richard West ('Favonius'), the dearest friend of the poet Thomas Gray at Eton. West believed that his mother had murdered his father; the idea preyed upon him and is thought to have been contributory to his early death. These would have been collaterals in whom Ivy might have delighted.

My novel *Stepsons* was the 'withheld novel', earlier mentioned. I was anxious that Ivy should read it in manuscript, for fear that it might not be published in her lifetime: it was a story of family tyranny that must appeal to her. She was persuaded to do this, some tactful excuse having been found; but finally it appeared in the year of her death, and her last letter to me acknowledged it.

A photograph taken at the Leeds ceremony reminds one of a Greek pediment, with the Princess Royal (Chancellor) and the

Vice-Chancellor as the central deities. Dr Compton-Burnett (as Roger Hinks remarked) contravened the 'law of frontality', presenting herself sideways to the camera.

I do not know where Henry Green picked up the erroneous information that Ivy had been a governess, but thinking of some of her sibylline utterances it was tempting to imagine her as a royal and imperial governess at Thebes and Mycenae. Queen Clytie might have written (in the style of royal letter-writers) to Jocasta Thebes: 'Darling Joc, in Burnett I am sending you a treasure. If Tiggy and Issy[3] love her as much as Iphy and Missy and Chryssy[4] did, you will have a very happy schoolroom.' There she could have seen what dreadful things happen in families. One may doubt if her influence on 'Missy of Argos' would have been altogether good.

[3] TRH the Princesses Antigone and Ismene of Thebes.
[4] TIH the Princesses Iphigeneia, Electra and Chrysothemis of Argos and Mycenae.

10

Now a new and delightful character must be introduced, Ivy's great friend Herman Schrijver. He was originally Margaret's friend, for his chief interest was interior decoration. I never met him, but my brother and I had a glimpse of him at Paddington in 1940, when he took Ivy and Margaret to Woodstock.

Elizabeth wrote of luncheon at Braemar Mansions:

Herman Schrijver was there, too. A nice man I had met more than once before. He kisses her on both cheeks. (In the Penn country one can tell who is anyone – it depends on whether a woman kisses Lady Curzon or not.) He flirts with her and flatters her. It is rather like being at the Court of Elizabeth I. He teases her. She answers him sternly and literally, but talks a great deal more and more fluently than usual. 'And you will not repeat what I have said, Herman. Once before I told you something that Angela Thirkell said, and you sold me to Edna [E. Box, the painter], who sold *you* to Olivia, who told someone else, who straightway wrote it in a letter to Angela herself. And I was very much blamed.' An ordinary person must have been put out by this. I expect that I should have burst into tears. Herman simply looked bemused. 'How frightful of me. But what a fascinating little chain it made.'

I usually take flowers, but this time took marrons glacés and she was much more pleased. She mentioned *Stepsons* and how

85

good she thought it, but Herman, not having read it, preferred
to talk about Muriel Spark. 'Not at all good,' Ivy said. 'I don't
like novels that tell you about *things.*'

Little Boswell notes.

'People should put their feet up more. I feel sure sitting
straight up is a Christian invention.'

'All children steal. I stole a pencil-box from my governess. I
simply looked her in the eye and said: "This is mine. If you had
one like it, you must have lost it." I kept it for years.'

'Apart from poor Henry, I really can't remember anyone I've
known committing suicide.'

The last remark is odd: her half-brother Charles certainly killed
himself by jumping off a bridge, and it is unlikely that the deaths of
her sisters 'Topsy' and 'Baby' were due to an accidental overdose
of veronal. Perhaps she preferred to forget them.

In May 1961 Elizabeth came again to Athens. This time, and during
subsequent visits, she stayed at 'Greek House' (as its English
proprietress called it) or 'Greek Home' (the name given to it by
her American partner). It is a pretty nineteenth-century house full
of strange alcoves and columns, in Kolonáki, the smart residential
quarter.

We went with George and his small sister Effie, and their
parents (the father as our driver) to Aegosthena, the beautiful
fourth-century fortress above an inlet of the Corinthian gulf that
protected the frontier between Attica and Boeotia. Elizabeth
watched with fascinated horror the forcible feeding practised on
the poor children. They were at an age when one often does not
like eating very much; and the Greeks, a poor race with memories
of starvation, like their children to be well fed, and to be seen to be
well fed. Their little noses were firmly gripped and *crema* (a sort of
milk pudding) was shovelled into their open mouths: they were
obliged to swallow or choke.

We also went with them to Perakhóra, a little port on the gulf, a factory of ancient Corinth on the opposite shore. Elizabeth had noticed the lighthouse on her flight back to England two years previously, and had marked it down as a place that she must see. 'To the lighthouse' had been our motto, and there we went, leading George, while the others made up a fire and roasted whole the lamb they had brought with them for a picnic luncheon.

Two things (apart from the forcible feeding) shocked Elizabeth in Greece: first the wasteful profusion of enormous unsold Easter eggs – for John was in the confectionery business and in England (it appears) such things are made to order; and then, the horrible way in which butchers hack up their meat, for in Penn she was exquisitely well served.

Her island trip that year was to Páros, perhaps the most successful that she ever made: it is the setting of her story 'In a Different Light'. The dog in it, I think, may have been taken over from Hydra.

She went with me to stay for two days with Mina Diamandopoulos and her son Alexis at their house on Poros. It is a white villa hidden in pine-trees in the tree-clad part of the island, Calavría. There is a small landing-stage to which one can take a caique from the port. The house and its lovely peaceful surroundings has been celebrated in *The Diblos Notebook*, the short novel by James Merrill.

We went for an excursion to the Peloponnesian mainland opposite. We saw the place where Theseus found the sword beneath the stone, at Dhamalà of Troezen, and we watched cheese dripping through a cloth to make myzithra. Back at the house we heard the song of a tree-frog.

Mina and Alexis had a guest in a tiny cottage behind their house, a rather cantankerous English poet. They told us that he had insulted most of their friends, and that he dearly loved a political argument. Forewarned, we dodged a conversation about 'political prisoners'; just as well, for his face was black with preparatory anger. Presently a remark of Elizabeth's started him off on capital punishment, because it emerged that Ivy was rather a friend to hanging. 'Did she know the statistics?' began the poet injuriously, longing to tell us what Sissy Jupe in *Hard Times* appropriately called the 'stutterings.' Elizabeth and I turned on him severely, and told him that someone who was both old and a distinguished writer was not to be bothered with such things. Although we routed him, he subsequently appeared on a terrace above that on which we were walking. Then our hostess appeared on a terrace higher still, put a large telescope to her eye, and read the time by the clock on the town tower. Delightful scene; it made Elizabeth think of Turgenev.

I had told Elizabeth that when my friends left Greece I always felt that they had gone into an underworld; I wanted them back, but had no wish to go with them. When I wrote to her after her departure she replied:

I was so glad to get your letter. It is the Underworld indeed, with rain slashing down out of a black sky, and the wind tearing the roses off the side of the house. We had some hot weather, but with an eiderdown of cloud under the sun. One of those days was last Friday, when I had a terrible time going to lunch with Herman to meet Ivy. There was a derailment on the railway-line ahead of our train and, after sitting fretting for forty minutes, we were all turned off it. Time was getting short and I ran in this awful heat to the nearest Underground, waited ages for a train, and then had an interminable journey into London. Ivy looked well and had just had a holiday in a private hotel [Broome Park, once the property of Lord Kitchener] in Kent. She was wearing black with a black straw hat with a deep brim like a laurel wreath. When Herman praised it, she said in an off-hand voice, 'Yes, they're all like that now.' But really she was out of humour. There were only four of us – the other the wife of the French attaché who kept talking about French literature while Ivy fidgeted with her bread and kept glancing at her chest. The smallest French phrase made her glower, and she hardly said a word. We had a delicious, cold, creamy, faintly

curry soup. She had hers hot. At least this pleased her. 'Hot soup
is so restoring,' she said. '*So restoring!*' cried Madame Maillot, or
whatever her name is. 'What a perfect expression! Who but
you could think of it?' This annoyed Ivy dreadfully. 'A perfectly
usual sort of word,' she snapped. 'I can think of no other.'
Herman asked me to tell them all about Greece – but I had
more sense than to do so. I knew that any more about abroad
would be too much. She even left her chocolate rum pudding,
although it was delicious, and I know she loves both ingredients.
'I love people who are specialists in a small field,' Herman said.
'People who know everything about some little subject, don't
you, Ivy?' 'No, I don't. They might try to tell me about it.' I
wish I had not such an account of grumpiness to give you. Not
once did we get that rather unwilling pursed smile, the sly
amused look down her nose. The soup seemed to fail in its
purpose, and so did Herman, in whom I would have put my
trust.

The next meeting was far better, just after the publication of
The Mighty and Their Fall (1961).

Herman Schrijver had Lesley Blanche [best known for her *The
Wilder Shores of Love*] and Ivy and me to lunch, and most amusing
it was. He is a deliciously frivolous man and Ivy responds to him
wonderfully. I don't often see her in outdoor clothes – she wore
a dark coat and skirt, a shantung blouse and a black straw hat.
Herman had two copies of her book for her to sign – one for
himself and one for a friend. 'I always write it on *this* page,' she
explained. 'Otherwise it looks as if it belongs to *me*.' 'Would
you write "To Charles" in this one?' Herman asked. 'No, I shall
do as I always do.' It was an exhilarating meeting with her,
because she was at her best and talking as she writes, and trying
not to smile when she made us laugh. We kiss now. Even saying
goodbye in the Brompton Road.

In the same year Elizabeth brought out *In a Summer Season*. She had let me see a draft of it, and I fancied that she had been a little timid about the dénouement, which was death in a motor accident, and feared that her own terrible anxiety over her son in the past might have inhibited her. I wrote:

Of course I didn't mean that the end of the book was very like your own experience, but I was afraid it might be too close for your comfort. Do you know the theory that Louisa Musgrove ought to have fallen out of a gig, but Jane Austen could not bear it because of poor Mrs Lefroy? . . . I daresay you can put in a little more shock as well as grief – it is very interesting, and not often done enough. . . . To return to the catastrophe of the Thorntons, it is basically all right, because you keep the rule that important characters who are going to die must begin dying from the start. Araminta is fey, and Dermot is 'hopeless', and their death is artistically right, and no one will bring in a verdict of wilful murder against you – although you have a strong motive to kill them. Dear Mr Forster is a homicidal author, I think – and I don't altogether acquit Ivy of Simon Napier's death [*More Women than Men*].

The whole book is a lovely evocation of that rare phenomenon, a really scorching English summer. It is the sort of book Elizabeth liked writing 'in scenes rather than narrative' – though at times she had difficulties with it. Once during its composition I wrote to her:

I fear your great cross is work having become weary, flat, stale and unprofitable. A heavy cross indeed, and don't I know it? There is nothing whatever to do about it, except, possibly, to put it down for a time. The great all seem to have had this cross to bear, and that is no comfort – I think more is to be found in the wicked suspicion that perhaps it's a thing those Snows haven't experienced.

The background tells more than the people or the happenings: the watersprinkler on the lawn; the hateful birds with their 'strident and spiteful noises' and 'those banal exchanges from tree to tree, mockings and bickerings and sudden solo trillings'; the cook with a napkin fastened round her head as if it were a Stilton cheese. . . .

It is a book full of minor felicities. Edwina, the worldly mother-in-law who goes in for interior decoration. 'My friend, Lord Auden and I cut one up the other day,' she says (of an old mahogany sideboard). 'We made a writing-table and two whatnots and a bedhead from it, and painted them all Adam green and white. We had a man sawing away for hours – great fun.'

There is Ethel and her cello, at which she saws away to the halting accompaniment of Lou, the schoolgirl niece. Ethel was once in gaol as a militant suffragette, and her friend Gertrude, 'another old lag', comes to stay. Gertrude is an absurd person who lives in a bird sanctuary ministering to 'oiled-up sea-birds' (Elizabeth got that from a charity appeal). The two 'old lags', who have read all about sex, have the most daring conversations about an experience they have never known at first hand.

Mrs Meacock is one of the author's most delightful servants, and the only one she 'goes behind' to reveal some of her thoughts. A good cook, evidently, though somewhat vulgarized by recent service with an American family who liked bits of pineapple all over things. She has a life of her own outside the kitchen, for she is compiling 'Five Thousand and One Witty and Humorous Sayings', and on most afternoons gives an hour to unravelling her material. For twenty years she saved up her money for the 'round trip', and having been round the world, is now full of memories. 'How you and Madam would love Bermuda. I can just picture you there. It is just Paradise on earth.'

It is a tale of two households: one consists of Kate, her young second husband Dermot, Tom, her son, Lou her daughter, and Ethel and Mrs Meacock. The other (the Thorntons) restored to life after long absence, consists only of Charles (widower of Kate's best friend) and his daughter, Araminta.

Mrs Meacock and Araminta had made a first appearance in a short story, 'The Prerogative of Love'. Araminta is a triumph. It is easy for a novelist to make a girl beautiful: he need only say 'let her be beautiful'. But Araminta is given a curious grace of movement and a gift for surprising which, as they owe nothing to the intellect, must have been excessively difficult to achieve. She is the sort of girl made to die in a motor accident (with another woman's husband), and the reader is not shocked when Dermot overturns a car with her and himself in it. She lingers through the night: Charles and Tom (who is in love with her) wait in the hospital. Kate sits up at home, Dermot being already dead. 'Charles and Tom returned together. It was beginning to be light and swallows, gathering to fly away, were noisy and busy round the eaves. She ran to the window and knew at once – from the way they shut the car doors and walked across the gravel – that Minty had died.'

Too much, it seemed to me, was made of Tom's grief: his courtship of Araminta was forward-looking, and deep grief needs roots in the past. Kate had lost a husband and Charles a daughter – the only child of her father and he a widower – and I thought them more worthy of compassion. But Elizabeth thought they would console each other, and ended with their marriage.

In 1962 she made an autumn visit to Greece. With 'the children' we visited the Amphiaraon, that lovely small tree-clad sanctuary in Attica. Suppose we were swallowed up by an earthquake, we thought, as Amphiaraus had been? What would happen to all our letters? We made another such excursion on to Mount Párnes, at its best season – it was still possible (indeed it is still possible today, though more difficult) to leave Athens and the world behind after a very few kilometres.

I think that it was during this visit that Peter Duval-Smith tacked on to us when we were going to dine at the Turkish harbour. He drunkenly ordered quantities of fish, which we were unable to eat, and for which he was not going to pay. Later we learned that he had gone back to London and given a mischievous account of our conversation in literary circles, and we were 'very much blamed'. He was in no state to form an idea of what we were talking about. He has since died a sad death at Saigon, choked in his own vomit after a bout of energetic drinking. This was our only common experience of the squalors of the literary world.

On her return – still a little dazed by Greece:

Everything here seemed so unreal that I had to come to terms with it as soon as possible, so that I can begin work. (The pen is weeping for me.) There is a curious feeling of walking on air, which I have never thought as agreeable a sensation as people try to make out.

I was so lucky, too. I came back to such a pretty St Luke's little summer – with pale blue skies and golden leaves and sunshine. But it scarcely lasted out St Luke, was awfully little, and today it is dark and cold. I was let down lightly at the beginning, though.

When I got back, I found a card from Ivy asking me to lunch – yesterday – Thursday; and John had written to Ivy to say he thought I could go, and so I did, and she was pleased to have the loukoumi. She was well and in good form, but unfortunately I never see her now without Herman Schrijver (John Pope-Hennessy was the fourth), and he is so frivolous and gossippy [sic] – which one would love in other circumstances – that Ivy never says anything interesting, and there are always the same conversations. The same food of *course* – the boiled bacon and parsley sauce and the white pudding. She carved up Muriel Spark and Iris Murdoch at the same time as the bacon. Marriage and religion were discussed and deplored. I felt guilty to be married and to have stayed married so long, and was almost thankful not to be religious. Rose Macaulay has never been forgiven. To have such a thing happen – when for a lifetime she had been a perfectly normal agnostic, like everybody else.

I discovered that Ivy cannot speak French. She had had a fan called Mrs Mayer to tea. 'Madame Mayer,' Herman corrected

her. 'I can't pronounce it the French way.' Ivy said. 'And she's
in *England* now.' She has been on holiday in Dorset (with a
friend who lives there), and in Shropshire and in Kent.
'Everybody goes to Greece,' she said scornfully – and rather
rudely I thought. After lunch, looking for some chocolates, she
went muttering round the room. I was terrified when Herman,
like someone in her books, turned to me and said: 'How
delightful it would be if one could hear what she's saying when
she does this. I can never hear anything.' She did not open the
loukoumi or the sweets that Herman took to her. We were
treated alike.

'Her clothes aren't good,' she said of Madame Mayer, when
told that she is rich. 'They are certainly ready-made.' This last
sentence sounded to me *so* governessy.

This letter was soon followed by another.

I'm afraid Ivy didn't say anything interesting about Murdoch
and Spark, except to say that the former is to be taken more
seriously – than the latter, not than she is. She agreed
energetically with me that she writes like Galsworthy. Herman
S. has just telephoned to ask me to go to the theatre with Ivy and
him next Thursday – to see Samuel Beckett's new play. This
should be a rather unusual outing. He told me that he had said to
Ivy that he hoped between the three of us we might make head
or tail of it, and she said, 'Well, we are three intelligent people,
so I can't see why we should have any difficulty.' I daresay *I*
shall. I wonder what she is like at the theatre. I don't think she
was pretending about the French. She seemed quite fussed about
it. . . .

The theatre was a matinée. After lunch with Herman. It was
a most enjoyable afternoon. . . . Herman gave me some pretty
match-boxes, and I said I would put one in Joanna's Christmas
stocking. 'My mother', Ivy said, 'told me that when I was a
child, she spent all the year looking out for small things to put in

my stocking. I remember those more than all the dolls I had – especially a little box of blue beads.' And her mother used to take her in a governess cart ('sometimes drawn by a donkey') to the seaside, when they lived in Essex. 'No more questions,' I say to people who ask them. So who would dare. But I asked one when we (they) were talking about income tax and rents and rates, and Herman implied that 95% was much the same as 100%. 'It is 5% different,' Ivy said impatiently. 'But could you work it out?' I asked. 'I have done so. I am very good at Arithmetic. When I was at school I was so good that I wasn't allowed to answer the questions, but had to give the other girls a chance.'

We had delicious food. The flat is full of . . . marble (hand-coolers and rulers and obelisks) and shutters for screens. . . . Frightfully dark, incense burning, and every space on the walls covered with pictures. 'Imagine dusting it,' Ivy said in the bedroom, as we put on our coats to go to the theatre.

Elinor [*sic*] Roosevelt had just died and I said how beautiful I thought the message Adlai Stevenson gave to the world. 'She would rather light a candle than curse the darkness.' 'Very good,' Ivy said. 'One would like it to be said of oneself.'

Well, then we went to the theatre (I am sorry to make such a letter of it, but is it not like going to one of the Basingstoke Assemblies with Jane Austen?). It was a sparse audience and Ivy took a great interest in it. 'Would you call it an *intellectual* audience, Herman?' (Too distinct voice in too empty auditorium.) 'One or two look that way inclined,' he whispered. 'Do you think they are staring at us, because they think *we* are intellectuals?' 'Of course they don't think that,' she said scornfully. 'We are *far* too well dressed.' 'Would it help if I took off my tie?' he asked. 'Not very much,' she – I think I will say 'retorted' for the first time in my life, 'for I daresay Elizabeth will have to take off everything.' So much for my intellectual underwear. The play – just the middle-aged woman buried in a mound – was to me quite unexpectedly wonderful – I went for

Ivy, and found myself forgetting her. She watched it keenly through opera glasses from the third row of the empty stalls, and I don't know how the poor actress carried on under the circumstances. '*Not* a play to miss,' she said in the interval, while Herman had gone running round Sloane Square to buy her a box of chocolates. *He* had dozed off in the first act, but always does after luncheon wherever he is, he explained. But I am sorry to say that, however alert Ivy's attention was and no matter how much Herman admired Brenda Bruce, they seemed to miss the point. It is really devastating, and as much as one can bear – a middle-aged woman's gallantry (I see so much of it) signifying the human tragedy – the terrifying attempts at optimism and the Molly Bloom nostalgia – heart-rendering.[1] 'Now is the crucial moment,' Ivy said, her hand wavering over the opened box of chocolates. 'One hopes for a ginger one. I wish your husband would make some good, *cheap* sweets,' she said, and then said – almost tenderly – 'he was very good to me in the difficult days'.

I am glad – as you must be – that she has her adoring courtier, to take care of her in her old age, and to give her gallantry and flattery and sweets. Not many women reach her years and have as much – for everything he can imagine her wanting he hastens to provide; and it is bestowed as if she were a young and lovely creature at her first ball, and when he helps her down the stairs or into a taxi – for she is getting frail – he turns her into Gloriana.

[1] A word of my Oxford servant.

11

Of *A God and His Gifts* (which came out in the autumn of 1963) Elizabeth wrote:

I too had enormous pleasure from Ivy's book, and loved the last line. I'm afraid she has lost her ear for baby-talk, though. She has done it much better, and there was such a quantity of it here; I dreaded the child coming in, as much as others must have done, but for different reasons. How marvellous, though, that she should grow more audacious as time goes on – the vastly public proposal and denunciations.

I had a letter from her this morning in which she said she had a bronchial chill and hoped that I fared better. 'But still take care. The evil days are on us. I hope we will meet when they are over.' It is like the Ides of March, and we had all better stay indoors. . . . The horoscope in the *Queen* prophesies disaster for nearly everyone I know on the 16th of this month (with the New Moon). We thought of having a party on that day to watch what happens to one another.

Elizabeth and I used with amusement to look at each other's horoscope in the newspapers, but without credulity: I explained to her that even if one believed in astrology they must be regarded as nonsense, being entirely unscientific and paying no attention to the

hour of birth and therefore to the 'rising sign'. But she had no wish
to go further into the pseudo-science, and did not know the hour of
her birth anyway – only that she had Sol in Cancer. So I would
congratulate her on her good prospects as a statesman, or she
would warn me of the dangers of dancing all night; but if the stars
looked down they would be no more likely to see her on a rostrum
than me on a dance-floor.

These are the pleasant sorts of games played by friends whose
friendship mainly lives by correspondence; to anyone else they
would just seem silly. Nor would a third person enjoy as much as
we did the dreams we liked to tell each other. I believe, coming
from so near the surface of consciousness they would not even be
interesting to science: our reading came so much into them. For
instance when in a dream she was conducted by me over a market
garden in Aegina, one could guess that she had been reading Angus
Wilson's *The Middle Age of Mrs Eliot*, in which a market garden
figures; or when I dreamed of a detective novel by her, with a
detective bearing her own name and very uncharacteristically
dressed there were signs of my addiction to the detective novels of
Gladys Mitchell. Elizabeth did not like detective stories, because
someone was usually hanged at the end of them.

She wrote again:

I went to see Ivy. She has bronchitis now, and her breathing is
laboured. It was a great shock to me to see her. I felt that I had
never seen anyone so old. Her hair is in two little plaits, and she
was wearing a rather dashing pink nylon night-gown. Quite a
surprise that. Her eyes look enormous – pale milky blue. She
was in marvellous form – exactly the same Ivy, talking a great
deal about money. And food. Though one would think not a
morsel had passed her lips for months. She took my hand, and
played with my bracelet – and her fingers, her wrist were just
bones. But the same pursed smile and mischievous sideways
glance, as if she really must not laugh at her own jokes. She was
discussing Truman Capote's *In Cold Blood* (which, in the middle

of the night, I wish I hadn't read). 'I find that nowadays I would much rather *not* read about criminals. They are so boring.'

I had told her that Ivy had had luncheon with Olivia Manning, and had written: 'She is always the same and always in a circle of the lettered. My own circle seems to come from several different worlds, one of them hardly literate.' I wondered whom that could consist of, perhaps her snob circle?

Elizabeth wrote:

I saw Ivy on Friday, but she did not mention anything – almost truly 'anything'. She was silent except for little violent outbursts about capital punishment and Iris Murdoch writing too much. Perhaps *we* (Herman Schrijver and a nice Dutch-woman) are really her hardly literate world. But there (at H.S.'s) the food is so beautiful that she applies herself to it. She did not know that I was to be there and came forward saying: 'My dear Elizabeth, what a very nice surprise. How thin you've become!' . . . She was in great good health and has traded in her Persian lamb for an ermine and almost pirouetted in it when admired. Well, Herman Schrijver says he will hire a car when the warm weather comes and drive her down to lunch with me in the Green Belt. . . .

Some undated scraps about Ivy.

I have just heard John Bowen [playwright and novelist] interviewing Ivy on the wireless. 'You write of the family as being a destructive unit.' 'I write of power being destructive and parents had absolute power over children in those days. Or one or the other had.' 'Especially, in your books, the father.' 'One or the other.' 'Miss Compton-Burnett, I'm afraid you may think this is an impertinent question' (I held my breath), 'but were there elements of that destructive power in your own family?' Her voice – high, floating and serene: 'No, no, there were not; but one saw it elsewhere. One saw it a great deal elsewhere.'

Mr Murray [John Murray, the publisher] said that he once asked Ivy if she had ever found *any* actual conversation of use in her writing. (Much braver than us, you see.) No, in all her novels, she had only used four sentences from life, deliberately lifting them, that is. I wonder which.

'I like growing old,' said Herman Schrijver.
'One goes on living and everyone else is dead,' Ivy remarked, spooning up lovingly late strawberries in a sabayon sauce.

Ivy, however, did not like friends dying; it made her angry if she felt they were leaving her too soon.
After the death of Roger Hinks I wrote to Elizabeth:

She wrote back most warmly and sympathetically – and on one sheet of writing paper made all the right points. She even had room to tell me that she had finished a short novel: 'but it suffered from my months of flat-hunting and threatened upheaval . . . stay in your flat. A move is a dreadful thing. And other flats are always worse'. She said that she had got 'quite dependent' on Roger – I suppose she may have known him for about thirty-five years.

Her rent having been enormously increased, because her landlord thought he could get much more from some South American tenants, Ivy began to consider moving. 'A nice thing if an English gentlewoman is to be turned out by Poles to make room for South Americans!' It would have been a distressing upheaval indeed – I think Elizabeth found 'Braemar' so depressing that she did not enter as deeply as I into Ivy's sufferings; she could not help hoping that a change might be for the better. Like Dr Johnson I am an enemy to change, and so was Ivy.

Finally I could write to Elizabeth:

Braemar has been saved. Olivia wrote to tell me that Ivy came
back (having found, at last, a suitable flat) and found a penitent
Polonaise willing for her to stay: 'at a great price, but less than
the South Americans'. She will sell capital and do so. 'I am at
home, and that is everything.' Be it never so gloomy – is there
still a sofa covered with black velvet? I am immensely relieved
– she had a terrible anxiety feeling, and the move might have
killed her altogether, and must have as a writer, I think.

We none of us, except perhaps Herman Schrijver, knew that Ivy
was quite well off, and that 'a dip into capital' did not mean ruin.
   It is things like that which are really destructive to writers, who
are often brave about illness and pain, and resilient after all but the
deepest grief. At this time Elizabeth had workmen in the house,
which is a great affliction. But it is not the worst thing that can
happen. She was in danger of losing her beloved Mrs Howard, who
might be setting up with a brother-in-law in a public house, and I
wrote:

I can't bear Mrs Howard to go. Awful for you to have no one.
To be stabbed in one's affections and left with piles of washing
up – I can't bear it. You will never have time to write another
line. It must not be. I remember Ivy telling me that she and
Margaret were ill for a fortnight when something of the sort
threatened them – and I doubt if they were also blasted in the
affections. . . . Shallow people (who eat in nasty restaurants)
do not know that these are the things that matter.

And again:

Dreadful for you to be without Mrs Howard – I was a day or
two without Maria, so I can completely sympathize. My
trouble, worse than washing-up, is the dust-bin. Maria ties up

the contents in parcels, and (I believe) exposes them on the hillside like unwanted infants. The dust-cart comes, like a sort of dead-cart, at a dead hour of the afternoon (irregular too) and rings a bell on the wrong side of the house, and cries: 'Bring out your rubbish.'

Elizabeth wrote:

Mrs Howard had an interview with the Brewers [her prospective employers] last night, but I do not wish to be writing about that. 'You realize you're ruining my Christmas,' I said to her. I might even say 'I hope you're satisfied now' – that bitterly unjust phrase. . . . It is kind of you to be so understanding about Mrs Howard's going – only another writer could be. 'You'll have to buckle to,' other people say. They relate experiences of 'being without anyone' for months at a time – as if my position is like theirs, with only housework to bother me.

Indeed 'being without anyone' is a misery far worse for a writer than bad reviews, or a nagging little illness, or a minor bereavement, or living under a bad government – Dorothy Osborne fared very well under the Commonwealth. And there is plenty to read and write even when there is strict censorship and the theatres are closed, so long as trustworthy domestic service gives one the time.

Fortunately Mrs Howard was with Elizabeth to the end. John, she said, once told her that for her three people could do no wrong: Mrs Howard, Elizabeth Bowen and the butcher. There was the implication that no one else could do much good.

In 1964 Elizabeth published *The Soul of Kindness*, one of her best novels. There are scenes in variety, but connected by an interesting theme and one that she made particularly her own, the self-deceiver. Her irresponsible Flora, who sees herself as 'the soul of kindness', and indeed is adored by people who see her in a very different light from that in which she sees herself, is (or would be, if she were allowed) catastrophic in her influence on other lives. She drives the wretched boy Kit, who has a platonic devotion to her, to attempt suicide by persistently upsetting him with ambitions for a stage career, for which he has no vocation. She has Emma's passion for matchmaking and continues to try to marry Kit's sister Meg to a novelist, Patrick Barlow – who is the type of homosexual who has very agreeable woman friends, but is in love with an odious, common boy with ginger hair. Here Flora has too much to contend with; but she does succeed in getting Percy, her father-in-law – one of those rich, plebeian businessmen this author does so well – to marry his mistress, Barbara. It is a great mistake: Barbara has to give up her small dress-shop and the cosy flat above where Percy liked to come round in the evenings; while Percy, lacking that place of resort, now leaves her alone and goes out to play billiards. Moreover, he finds it a nuisance to have her in his flat all day, when he wants to do piano practice, or to play at conducting an orchestra.

Elizabeth wrote somewhere: 'I think loneliness is a theme running through many of my novels and short stories, the different ways in which individuals can be isolated from others – by poverty, old age, eccentricity, living in a foreign country – even by having committed murder, as in *A Wreath of Roses* (there are several kinds of loneliness in that novel).'

In *The Soul of Kindness* there are even more. Flora's mother, Mrs Secretan, after a beautiful wedding for her daughter, lives alone in the Green Belt haunted by a fear (found to be baseless) of cancer: a double solitude, being alone and shut up with fear. Her eccentric housekeeper Miss Folley ('Ah, Folley, rightly named!' Ivy might have said) fills her empty life by writing fantastic love-letters to herself which she reads to her employer. Elinor Pringle – Flora's neighbour – grass-widowed by her husband's political work and his play-writing, fills up her time at the cinema or in provincial towns, and sits alone in melancholy pubs. Patrick Barlow paces about his flat, where parchment coloured silk curtains shut out the view of the congregational chapel, waiting in on the chance that Frankie may turn up.

'Situations', Elizabeth wrote, 'I have sometimes taken from life, as a jumping-off point: but imagining myself into another world, using the eyes of the people I am creating is what my writing has chiefly been about.'

Like Mrs Secretan, Elizabeth had married off a daughter, like her she had lived in fear (then unfounded) of cancer, and had felt uncomfortably sure that she had offended someone; like Elinor Pringle she had filled up time in odd places, during short periods of being alone; like Meg, she knew the fascination of the Thames estuary; with Patrick Barlow she shared the accidie of the writer, and a love for the same sort of painting. But she was not at all like any of these people, and the experiences in the book are theirs and not hers. And I am sure she knew that when the alternative to loneliness is boredom, which is frequently the case, loneliness is much to be preferred.

Flora, always spoilt, is never lonely – until at the last she has the frightening experience of seeing herself as one pair of hostile eyes saw her: the eyes of a person so ill-conditioned as to send her an anonymous letter, and yet a painter of distinction. At all times Flora is supported by her devoted cook Mrs Lodge, who has disquieting attacks of nostalgia for the country, but seems doomed to stay for ever in suburbia. Sometimes I have wondered if Elizabeth, for once the contrary of Jane Austen, had said to herself: 'I shall make a heroine whom no one but I shall dislike.' If this were so, I think she too capitulated to Flora.

12

It was at Easter (a late Greek Easter) that Elizabeth came to Greece in 1964. Together we watched the beautiful funeral procession of the Dead Christ on Good Friday, and its station in Kolonáki Square; and on the following night we waited by the reservoir till midnight to watch Lycabettus coming out in pinpricks of light all over, as the Easter candles were lit. Elizabeth, though not in the least religious, liked the ceremonies and seasonal activities of the Orthodox Church, but when the weather was unseasonable she wished the clergy would put nylon coverings over their handsome vestments.

On Easter Monday we went with 'the children' and their party to see the panegyri at Arachova, near Delphi. St George's day, the village feast, is transferred to Easter Monday if 23 April falls in Lent. We lingered too long in Livadià on the way, by the charming waters of memory and forgetfulness, and were too late to see the sports at Arákhova, with the very old men running to win a lamb as a prize.

Elizabeth's island trip was to the beautiful, calm, olive-grown island of Sifnos. 'It's Hickie Borman's job to get you there,' John had said, naming her travel agents. And they got her there.

After her return to darkness and rain – not that she was generally very lucky in her weather in Greece – Elizabeth wrote:

I met Herman at the FitzGeralds' [the writer Kevin FitzGerald and his wife Janet – the latter had been Herman's producer on the occasions when he broadcast on *Woman's Hour*], and he says that there is less of Ivy every time he sees her. And she is forgetful. Olivia Manning went to tea with her, and Ivy said to Herman afterwards, 'I don't know what mistakes I made. I was under the impression all the time that she was Elizabeth Taylor.' How delighted Herman was you can imagine. He said that on her birthday[1] he asked her what she had learnt from life, and she thought for a long time, and then said: 'That people are morally the same, and intellectually different.'

He said that he had never heard of 'the place' [the seat of Compton or Burnett ancestors]. She had never mentioned living anywhere but in Hove, until she came to London to live with Margaret. They were introduced to one another by a woman friend who thought they should get on well in London as Margaret came of a better family and knew the people, and Ivy had the money. He insists that she has always had plenty.

Herman says that her sisters have deliberately been kept from him. He is also sure that she has hardly been educated at all.[2] 'All that talk of coming between brothers and so on – but she cannot speak a word of any language but English, and is furious if one says the smallest phrase in French.' This, I had already guessed.

He said that after he came back from Margaret's funeral, to which she didn't go, she seemed quite stunned and sat staring in front of her, and saying 'I've lost my man', over and over again. For some reason, I find this very difficult to imagine.

Of course Herman loves her whisperings – for he is always convinced that he will catch a word or two – but all he has ever heard was when she was going from the dining-room to the drawing-room after lunch with him, and she whispered: 'I hate sauces. I hate sauces.' 'And that I am sure I was meant to hear,' he said.

When he first knew her, when she was plump and big-boned,

[1] Ivy's eightieth birthday was on 5 June 1964.
[2] We know from Mrs Spurling's book that she was very well educated.

and had that corn-coloured hair and always wore pale grey, she would sit at Margaret's parties and never say a word.

I think he fears she will die soon – is already fading away.

Another undated scrap about Ivy must date from about this time, when she still invited people to luncheon:

She, too, holds up the spoon and tries to tempt me. She does it especially to me. The young-old men from Sotheby's escape this attention. I think she is trying to console me with food for not being a very good writer. When she fills up my glass with water – for there is not always wine – it is a protective and consoling gesture.

Elizabeth came to Greece again in 1966. That summer her island trip was to Thásos, and I was particularly glad that she would go there as it entails flying to Kaválla, which can be the most desirable flight that a woman can make in Greece. Either going or coming one should cross the Athos peninsula and look down into monasteries on the Holy Mountain that no female eye may otherwise see. Of course one may have bad luck, and a less interesting route may be taken, and I fear that happened to her. I remember that she asked me to guess what was inside a sort of pasty served to her on Thásos, and that I got it right at the first guess: macaroni. Otherwise she had only praise for the beautiful island.

We made the excursion with 'the children' that had become traditional; perhaps it was the most beautiful, and it was to be the last. We drove through forest and isolated villages and then, after a final stretch of dull road, to the sanctuary of Nemesis at Rhamnus – the least visited, I suppose, of Attic sites. It is less spectacular than many, there is little more than broken masonry, but though there are many more dramatic landscapes, there can be few so utterly Hellenic. The hills fall to the sea in gentle contours, exactly as they should; there is woodland and cliff, and part of the outline

of Euboea across a blue strait. It is a place of calm and classical
beauty: I am afraid it is exactly the sort of place for which one
must long most desperately when out of Greece.

She never set foot in Greece again. On 21 April 1967 the
'Colonels' Revolution' took place. Elizabeth was among the
many people who felt disinclined to come here during that regime;
twice, indeed, she sat, like Maurice Bowra, on deck at Piraeus.
'We did not wish to be speaking of it', though of course I regretted
our separation. Later, I believe, it was taken out of her hands for,
having said something disobliging in an interview, she was
blacklisted, and another woman of the same name had difficulty in
entering the country. For Elizabeth, as for many other philhellenes,
it was a real sacrifice and to be respected; but those of us who lived
and worked here were grateful to writers who did not join in the
boycott – to John Bailey, Francis King, Peter Levi, Lady
Longford, Nancy Mitford, Iris Murdoch, Barbara Pym, Muriel
Spark and others. After all, the boycott punished those whom
there could be no intention to punish, and it made no difference to
tourism, which boomed during those years.

Meanwhile, Ivy was made a Dame. She was pleased at the
distinction, and amused, as she told me, that twice she had been
decorated by a Labour government; she almost felt she ought to
vote for them! But Margaret knew nothing about it, and therefore
she could hardly feel that she was a real Dame.

In the winter she fell and broke her thigh, for the second time.
Elizabeth wrote:

I too went to see Ivy before she left hospital. The Sister sent me
to her room, but she wasn't there. 'She's gone to the loo,' a
Nurse said. How disrespectful, I thought. I took her some
Loukoumi and chocolates, and she said, 'Now that *is* a sensible
present.' Then in came a basket from Fortnums, which I helped
her to open. Inside were six large oranges. 'Oranges! Well, I did
ask him for tangerines. I daresay oranges will be very nice,
though. How greedy everyone must think me. My sisters sent

me a melon, but there was so much else, that in the end it had to be given to people in the wards.'

Tea was brought in. 'Here you are, poppet,' the nurse said. 'They call me "poppet" and "sweetie-pie" and things like that,' Ivy said smiling. I always thought nurses were a tough crowd. 'How I long to be at home and have some *plain* food. I know *you* understand. A baked potato and some porridge, you know.'

We must not believe a word that Herman says, for she described her Christmas stocking differently, and with some pleasure. 'It had little sensible inexpensive things in it – a folding coat-hanger and something to put on one's face. . . . Ah, well, the nurses enjoyed it all, and that was what it was for. Some of the patients were very groggy afterwards, though.'

Of Miss M's book [Olivia Manning's *Friends and Heroes*], she said, 'Very well she did it, I thought. But I hope she won't go *on* doing it.'

She has gone home now. Perhaps just as well. 'This is all coming out of capital,' she said, looking gloomily round the gloomy room.

If I have said comparatively little about Elizabeth's short stories, it is not at all from lack of admiration though, like Ivy (I think), I very much prefer the novel as a form. It is moreover difficult to place them in roughly chronological order, for the date of composition or publication was often much earlier than the date when they were collected. Elizabeth Bowen wrote: 'A writer of short stories is at his or her best sometimes, and sometimes not; and this is equally true at any age or in any year at which he or she happens to be writing. "Development" may appear in any one writer's successful novels; in successful stories, I hold it to be a myth.'[3] And indeed it may be doubted if Elizabeth Bowen ever wrote a more beautiful story than the early 'Joining Charles'.

Nevertheless it may be said that Elizabeth Taylor was more

[3] *Pictures and Conversations*, p. xxii.

often at her best in each successive collection of stories, though I do not know that she ever surpassed the brilliant study of deception in the title story of *A Dedicated Man*. The 'germ' of this story, I think, is the idea (I do not know who first expressed it) that couples of servants who apply for situations as man and wife have often met for the first time in the registry office. It could not have been better developed.

Her next novel, *The Wedding Group* (1968) is a study of a different sort of deception. Midge, the most important character, is a middle-aged woman clinging to a bachelor son, himself already in early middle age. She welcomes a mistress who is not likely to take him from her, even a waiflike wife who shares his dependence on her. Midge holds her son and her daughter-in-law by cupboard love, having become an excellent cook – ironically, her husband abandoned her in part because the food was so bad. She is (I think) the only one of this author's deceivers who is finally caught out. She may deserve it, and yet the reader pities her failure with her three generations of men – her father, her husband and her son – and is sorry that her grandson will be taken from her.

As always, Elizabeth shows herself a thoroughly English writer in her sensitiveness to the vagaries of the weather and to minor class distinctions; and whatever Dr Johnson may say about the unimportance of the former or contemporary prigs about the latter, they contribute so much to the variety of life and conversation in England. Of three of the principal women, Midge and Alexia so clearly belong to different classes, and Cressy to none.

Cressy, the waiflike wife, is a refugee from a strange Catholic family community dominated by a patriarchal grandfather who as an artist has something of Holman Hunt (I fancy) as well as of Eric Gill, who more immediately inspired him. The rather touching absurdity of their homespun life is faithfully done, and Cressy's longing for the modern world of discothèques and Wimpy bars. She is an entirely successful creation: an individual, and yet very much the result of her origins.

There are other admirable characters, particularly the devoted brother and sister, Toby and Alexia, who keep an antique shop and are as happy as anyone can be in fact or fiction – they employ Cressy, and in their shop is the Wedgwood wedding group. There is also Midge's deserting husband who left her, not for another woman, but just left her, and went to keep house for an invalid aunt.

In the same year I published *The Deep End*. Ivy, who did not much care for books about 'Abroad' – though if you sent her one she would say politely that it would be 'a companion' – was pleased to have a novel set in England and in the past. She congratulated me on eschewing the filth and violence that at that time were almost necessary to sell a book (as my publisher told me), and said that she almost felt that she might have written it herself. But what was most interesting was her praise of the *good* characters. The goodness of her own good characters was a thing she always insisted on, and felt to be imperfectly appreciated. I remember how grudgingly E.M. Forster once wrote to me that he knew Ivy's characters were good as well as clever; they are a great deal better than anyone in his books.

Elizabeth and I corresponded as usual, though there was no immediate likelihood of our meeting; but we were used to that. It seemed just possible that we might meet in Menton, where she went as judge for the Katherine Mansfield Prize – an inappropriate meeting-place, for we both greatly disliked 'K.M.' She was to inspire the admirable story 'Sisters' in Elizabeth's next collection – the story of a cosy, bourgeoise, widowed ex-mayoress in a provincial town being embarrassed by questions about her famous, disreputable sister.

Elizabeth's travels now took her to Corsica, and she almost hesitated to tell me that she found Calvi more beautiful than Greece. But it was her North African journeys that were to give her two short stories, and she wrote with enthusiasm of the beautiful *tajines* she had eaten in Morocco. Greek food, not surprisingly, she preferred to enjoy at the White Tower restaurant in Soho.

13

There was not much more written about Ivy. In the summer of 1969 she seemed to be taking leave of us all, and the last letter I had from her, thanking me for my novel *Stepsons* – which she called *her* book – was like a valediction. When she had seen it earlier in manuscript she had written: 'It fulfilled my highest hopes, and they were high. And I am enjoying the sense of peace that comes from the feeling of gaps filled and curiosity satisfied.' I could feel that my friendship with her had come full circle.

At the end of August Herman telephoned to tell Elizabeth that Ivy was dying. She died very quietly next day, 29 August. On that day (and I should like to think at that very hour) I was standing, in all ignorance, at the end of the Appian Way in Brindisi, under the tablet commemorating the death of Virgil. I have never managed to adapt the epigram to Ivy: *Pinner me genuit, Braemar rapuere. . . .*

Alethea Hayter (author of *Opium and the Romantic Imagination*, who was for many years with the British Council) broke the news to me a week or so later, when I stopped off in Corfu to see her, on my return journey to Athens. She showed me *The Times*, with the story of the half-dozen looking-glasses.

'I hope she left you one,' said Alethea.

'I don't expect so,' I said. 'She didn't trust "Abroad" – she wouldn't want a fragile object sent abroad.'

On my return home that night I was astonished to find a copy of her will sent me by her solicitors, Mowll and Mowll, and to find that I was one of Ivy's six residuary legatees. I had always imagined her to be rather badly off; she often wrote as if her increased rent would be her ruin. Had I thought about her will, I should have expected her to leave everything she had to members of her family, like most people of her generation. In consequence I was altogether taken by surprise – and, as I confessed to Elizabeth, at first it was the thought that I valued, though I knew Ivy would want me to value the money more. But I had the thought at once, and at a moment when I was depressed, and it could not be devalued. Kay Dick has written that Ivy left the residuary legatees £10,000 each, and I dare say she hoped she was leaving us £5,000; but after tax was paid we got little more than half the latter sum. Nevertheless, such a generous and unexpected gift must have been valued by all of us, and not only as a proof of the affection that prompted it. I believe there was considerable jealousy among those who had not been so fortunate.

Here is another undated scrap from a letter of Elizabeth's:

A woman at a party . . . who is famous for her condescensions, was telling me how very silly she considers it that some women are not satisfied to stay at home, but must range all over the world looking for adventures. Unlike me. I am the admirable type of woman – 'You look after your home and your husband and children, and you have your little hobby and that keeps *you* busy.' I smiled the sort of smile that was meant to express gratitude and modesty, and disclaim any right to her kind praises. As my glance strayed over her grey hair, I was really thinking 'You are exactly my age, and you look far older, I think, and you are extremely fat and you don't look at all nice in that dress and anyhow you're a South African, and I am sorry for your children, not that I like them either, and everyone knows that your boorish husband drinks like a fish. . . . I shall just boycott her – along with the tinned peaches and South African sherry I should also boycott if I had ever bought them anyhow.'

For Elizabeth was a completely serious professional writer, though I am sure that she disliked the interviews and activities that are often imposed on successful authors, and she always wished to keep her personal life detached from the mafia of the literary world. To one questionnaire she replied, as she told me, that her private life was not only her own, and she therefore very properly refused to say anything about it. All the same, I do not think she minded giving her opinions on general subjects if she were asked, though she approved of my formula: 'I am not in the habit of giving my opinion on subjects that I have not particularly studied, and on which I can claim no authority' – not that I should waste a stamp on replying.

She was amusing about her admirers: the Scandinavian woman who remembered her books far better than she did herself, and came to see her and said: 'This is the view from *In a Summer Season*'; or the Japanese who asked her what she considered the 'high point' in her 'fructuous career'. She had hostile letters too; for example, that from a person who likened her to a 'temple dancer'. One cannot imagine what he meant, but it did not seem to have been intended as a compliment.

Despite her affection for Ivy, she was never a part of the 'Braemar gatherings'; but before and after Ivy's death she frequently lunched with Herman Schrijver, and was a comfort to him during his long and hopeless illness. He had been given four months to live by the doctors, and very much exceeded that allowance – always brave and cheerful and amusing, and offering an example that only too soon Elizabeth was to follow. He delighted in her company, and told her that having so little time left he was not going to waste it with people whom he did not like – so much more honest and sensible than people who say 'Life's too short to quarrel in'.

The only interruption in my correspondence with Elizabeth was during the long postal strike of 1971. It was a fortunate coincidence that if my right hand had to be incapacitated for writing by some sort of disc trouble it should be just at that time. I do not know how this came about, or how a physiotherapist, with almost indescribable torture, managed to put it right after some months.

In consequence it was all the more maddening that we just missed each other in Cyprus in the spring. I was with a friend in hideous Famagusta, while she and John were in the Dome Hotel at Kyrenia – a last outpost of empire. She had spoken of going, but I had believed it would be later than I was able to go, and perhaps the confusion between the dates of Western and Orthodox Easter was in part to blame.

In this year, 1971, she published her beautiful novel *Mrs Palfrey at the Claremont*, a sad, tender and amusing story of old age. Mrs Palfrey, a widow, makes her home in a residential hotel in the Cromwell Road where the elderly residents are treated as second-class clients by the bumptious manager – 'they aren't allowed to die there'. It is stuffy and claustrophobic, but they cling on for all they are worth: they have lost their homes, and have nothing to look forward to but a geriatric ward or the grim Braemar nursing home.

In such a limited world each has to keep his end up, and the newcomer Mrs Palfrey soon realizes that it is visitors that confer prestige. Unfortunately she has mentioned a grandson in the British Museum, but he never comes near her. Then an occasion enables her to practise a touching deception. She falls down on a pavement and is befriended by Ludo, a penniless and charming young man, and invites him to dine at the hotel. It is assumed by fierce old Mrs Arbuthnot that he is her grandson Desmond, and so Desmond he has to be. The tangled web she has woven is in danger when, for once, the real Desmond appears; but Mrs Palfrey dies (not in the Claremont) unexposed, and befriended to the last by Ludo.

There is a fine supporting cast of minor characters: the vulgar, bibulous Mrs Burton; the superior Lady Swayne who comes for an annual visit, condescends to the residents, and shows off to them about her frequent engagements with the friends on whom she inflicts herself; the appalling Mrs de Salis who settles into a flat and invites her former messmates (if so one may call them) to a dreadful party with red and white 'plonk', and a very much retired actress as an attraction; and Mr Osmond, missing the world of men where he can tell improper stories, who takes Mrs Palfrey to a Masonic dinner, and suggests marriage and a common flight from the Claremont to a home of their own where they can give wine and cheese parties.

But others have their pathos: the crippled, suffering and fierce Mrs Arbuthnot, and humble Mrs Post, who is only too glad to run errands for her. They do not pretend not to be old. Mrs Arbuthnot cannot, for she has become incontinent and almost incapable, and has to go off to die in the Braemar. The whole depressing atmosphere of empty lives and small economies is touchingly conveyed: the little solitary walks; the changing of library books; the daily inspection of the menu posted by the lift door. The one distraction lacking is church. I remember passing some weeks in childhood at such an hotel, perhaps a few doors from the Claremont. There was much talk about church: St Stephen's was too high, St Jude's too low, and St Peter's about the right level. But their notices seem to have been posted up in the Claremont, near the menu.

It is not surprising that *Mrs Palfrey* was a brilliant success on television, with Celia Johnson in the title role. Elizabeth and John went to luncheon with the actress in very different circumstances from those in which Mrs Palfrey had to do her entertaining. She gave them venison killed by her own forester – when I heard this I felt England was still standing where she stood of old.

In the summer of 1972, returning to Athens for a few days between two journeys, I was horrified to hear from Elizabeth that she had just had a cancer operation. It was at 'St Jo's': St Joseph's Home at Beaconsfield, a delightful establishment run by Irish nuns – 'you aren't allowed to die there'. She knew it as a visitor; a friend had gone there for her confinement, and was rewarded with cries of 'Holy Mother of God, what a smashing baby!' Another friend had a smoked trout brought in by his wife, and one of the sisters absent-mindedly fried it. She was a Cassius Clay fan, it was explained, and all her thoughts were on 'the big fight'. While Elizabeth was at St Joseph's there were burst pipes. No useful man among the patients, a sister complained, all 'retired'; true, there was an engineer, but he was only half an hour off the operating-table. Elizabeth wrote a short story while she was there, and sold it for £1,000.

That autumn she went on a cruise with John in an Italian boat. She would not disembark in Greece, so I went to Iráklion in Crete to see her, as this was the only chance. Her cruise ship and my boat from Piraeus sailed into the harbour at exactly the same time, eight o'clock in the morning. I breakfasted with them, and we sat on deck in the sun. Most of the cruisers had gone to see the museum, but they had both seen it in time past. It was a great comfort to feel that we were not eternally separated, and we went on talking as if nothing had happened for a long comfortable morning. She seemed in good health, though the motor journey to join her ship had been a great strain.

Even when Ivy was still alive we had had Ivy jokes and games. Elizabeth's daughter Joanna, when still a child, had delighted us by picking up Elizabeth Bowen's story, 'Ivy Gripped the Steps', and remarking: 'What an extraordinary thing for her to do!' While I had seen an article in *Vogue* headed 'How to train ivy to become festive'.

Now we invented dialogues on themes from contemporary life that had not come Ivy's way: she might have done much with sex change.

'"Your father has returned," said Mrs Wordsworth, "But he is no longer your father. He has become a lady."

'"He could not," said Dorothy. "One must be born a lady. He might become a woman."'

Or there was the new cannibalism: flying over a desert in Persia, I had looked round the aeroplane and wondered which of my fellow-passengers I could most easily bring myself to eat if I survived an air-crash. One could imagine 'A Family at a Feast'.

The following summer she and John made another cruise, and we were to meet in Piraeus. By chance I spent a few days' holiday in Myconos just before, and found that her boat was to put in. I hoped to take her by surprise. This proved to be impossible, but it was a satisfaction to send her a note 'see you on Thursday' (or whenever it was), as if it were the most ordinary thing in the world.

'The children' came down to Piraeus to see Elizabeth again, and stayed on, though I had not intended it. However, we could leave them to their own devices and go on talking. Now it seemed that the barrier did not matter; it was only regrettable that time was short, and the cruisers must have been allowed only a very rapid visit to Athens.

In the meantime Elizabeth had been again in North Africa, and on setting out had been deeply saddened by the death of her friend Elizabeth Bowen. Now, I told her, there was only Mrs Howard who could do no wrong – the butcher had died long ago, his last task for her being the hanging of a beautiful sirloin that Elizabeth took to the Derby, and we said of him that he was now 'forever with the Lamb'. His place had in some measure been taken by his assistant Sammy, the greater artist. Elizabeth Bowen left a place that could not be filled, though I now had the honour to share with Mrs Howard the inability to do wrong.

I do not think Elizabeth was ever really robust again, but there was a great deal of happiness still in store for her – a delightful holiday with her daughter in the Dordogne, and above all her happy times with her grandchildren, for if anyone understood the art of being a grandmother it was she. On the other hand a broken marriage in the family gave her great pain and anxiety. Nevertheless, when I went down to Piraeus to see her again in the summer of 1974 I had no idea that we were to lose her so soon.

She and John had been on a cruise on a Turkish boat, and the death of a fellow-passenger when they had arrived at Istanbul may have been the first germ, as it was the starting-point, of her last

novel, *Blaming*, published after her death. She had, I think, begun it
before cancer struck again in the autumn. In the beginning it was
an affection of the throat that made her almost speechless, or able
to talk only in whispers. From the first it was feared that this was
connected with her earlier illness, and so it proved to be. She was
determined to have her family Christmas and to 'do her old
Capulet stuff' – once she told me that she did not want to be like
Juliet's mother, and I told her she was much more like her father,
always so much concerned about the catering.

By the New Year there was little doubt that she was gravely ill.
She was always brave and amusing, determined to take one day at
a time and not to indulge hopes or fears. Soon she said that she did
not wish to be speaking of it, but she promised to tell me if any
'dramatic' change occurred.

She went on working on her novel. I do not think it shows haste,
though I do think that she saved time – in the only artistic way
possible – by deliberately keeping it rather bare. She had
preferred Ivy's work when it was less bare than in *A Heritage and Its
History*, and I can imagine how much she might have enjoyed
developing such a character as the Reverend Patrick Padstowe
(and how much we should have enjoyed the development), had she
had time for inessentials. She might also have told us a little more
about Nick as a painter, although she has really told us enough.

Once he painted a rather grand lady walking in a park with a
cardigan hung over her shoulders, her head bent, her arms like
this . . . her face hardly showing; beautiful trees going away
into the distance, two horses grazing. . . . Nick thought she
might be annoyed or disappointed; but everybody loved it, and
then everybody wanted to be set down in their own
surroundings. And the Duchess said, 'Now I can walk in my
own park forever.'

The subject of the book is named in the title: blaming, of oneself,
of others, of circumstances. Amy, whose husband Nick dies on

board ship at Istanbul, has at first to blame herself – as the survivor of any close union must, however blameless – for her shortcomings and impatience. Then, of course, she has the cruelty of life to blame.

An American fellow-traveller, Martha, who has made friends with Amy and Nick, generously deserts the ship to take care of Amy at this crisis. Back in London, Amy is ungratefully unwilling to see Martha, who reminds her too vividly of her tragedy. For this she is blamed by her son (always unstinting of blame) and very much more gently by herself. Her son James also blames her for extravagance in keeping on a house that is too big for her. This is one of the causes for a growing parsimoniousness, which is shamed by Martha's careless generosity.

Martha makes a somewhat ill-considered marriage with Simon, who takes her back to the States, where he is a lecturer at a provincial university. She leaves 'escape money' with Amy, who is to send her an aeroplane ticket if she cannot bear her new life. Of course she cannot, and the escape is made. Amy selfishly does not go to meet her at the airport, as she knows she ought (and as James does not fail to point out). The next news she has of Martha is her suicide. James does at least get his mother to the crematorium, and afterwards there is a painful scene with Simon, who wants to repay Amy for the air ticket, having known nothing of the 'escape money'. He bitterly blames himself, and Amy warns him against self-censure; some she feels herself, if not quite enough.

The book is sometimes painful reading for those of us who knew and loved Elizabeth: we cannot help feeling that she is exposing an old wound and exorcizing the ghost of her friend Maud, who mysteriously 'escaped' from New Zealand, saw no one, and flew back and committed suicide. Elizabeth should in no way have blamed herself, for she had left nothing undone. She would have been incapable of Amy's selfishness – at most she may have regretted that a letter of hers failed to arrive in time. It is no doubt our own fault if we let ourselves be troubled: Martha is not at all like Maud, nor Amy like Elizabeth; and Amy's reactions are largely due to the shock of widowhood. Elizabeth knew that suffering does not improve most people.

There is an interesting set of minor characters, despite the comparative bareness of the book. Gareth Lloyd, the excellent doctor, never blames. He is a widower, and will become Amy's second husband, to the great relief of her son. There is a new sort of servant, Ernie Pounce, an amusing but hypochondriac ex-sailor. Above all, there are the grandchildren, full of the demonic and mutual jealousy of the young. And here is the saddest personal touch.

'I think I've forgotten Grandpa too,' said Dora, revisiting Nick's studio some time after his death.

So much for early memories, Amy thought. And she loved him so much.

Here, I think, she was facing a large part of her own tragedy.

In the summer of 1975 Elizabeth had a 'remission', and John motored her to Alsace; but disappointingly she was very ill, and they had to make an early return. Then she was well enough to enjoy the beautiful summer and even to bathe in Joanna's swimming-pool. Joanna had a delightful party for her birthday on 3 July, and the French student lodging with her wrote with admiration of the quantity of wine consumed at the 'Fête de la mère de Madame'. In an essay on English food he had written: '. . . the English always have bread and water on the table; but they do not eat the bread or drink the water'.

For some time the friendship of Kingsley Amis and his wife, Elizabeth Jane Howard, had meant very much to her; she and John often exchanged visits with them. They were such easy people to entertain, for they dropped off to sleep after luncheon. Late in

August they went over to Penn, and Jane Amis lay down and drew the curtains. Anxious neighbours rang up to ask if Elizabeth were very ill – 'and I am very ill,' she wrote, a characteristic way of introducing bad news. John had constantly been motoring her over to Norwood for very tiring treatment, and I know she was in much greater pain than she cared to mention.

Now, she said, she cared no more for food or drink, not even gin or 'the best Evesham asparagus', and she felt strange in not planning her 'old Capulet stuff' for Christmas. But she was profoundly thankful to be surrounded by the most perfect love and care, unlike poor Elizabeth Bowen who had to pass so many of her last months in loneliness.

Soon she was almost always in bed; she rejected a treatment that made the hair fall out: 'I refuse to be a bed-ridden crone in a crooked wig.' And Mrs Howard told her not to let 'them' make a guinea-pig of her. She could hardly write, and the electric typewriter John brought her was too heavy – and it was never an instrument with which she had felt happy. But her last letter, written on this machine, was brave as ever. In it she told me a funny story about Ivy out of a book of memoirs.

She died on 19 November 1975, on her 'name-day', the feast of St Elizabeth of Hungary, a woman whom she in no way resembled, and a martyr to 'blaming' of herself, and to blame from her spiritual director. Few people can have had as little reason as Elizabeth for self-censure, and I hope that in her last book – which at least she saw in proof – she got rid of any such feelings she ever had. As Tory said in *A View of the Harbour* (though Maud said it first): 'Novelists recover.'

Novelists recover indeed from grief and pain and shame and embarrassment (less completely from the last – there are 'places on which one locks a door and turns one's back'). This does not mean that they recover from the consequences – loss.

These two wonderful friends had in a measure made up to me for being *sans famille*. To Ivy I almost felt as a nephew (and like E.M. Forster I descend from 'a long line of maiden aunts', a proud pedigree). To Elizabeth I felt almost as a brother, the more so that we had Ivy in common as an aunt; and while she lived Ivy remained more living to me.

I still want to ask Elizabeth questions, constantly think of things I want to tell her and worse – perhaps – I find too many things not worth doing because I cannot write to her about them. I have deliberately lingered over the sorting of our letters and the writing of these pages, for this has been like a prolongation of our long correspondence.

Nevertheless I know how fortunate I have been in enjoying a long, cloudless, unbroken friendship with Elizabeth and Ivy. It is a possession for life, and I thank God (in whom they did not believe) on every remembrance of them.

BIBLIOGRAPHY

In the listings below, the original publishers and dates of publication are given. Subsequently many of the novels by Elizabeth Taylor and Ivy Compton-Burnett have been reissued by their original and other publishers. The books by Robert Liddell do not include his translations of the works of certain Greek writers. Except where an alternative place-name is given, all of these titles were first published in London.

ELIZABETH TAYLOR

Angel, Peter Davies, 1957.

At Mrs Lippincote's, Peter Davies, 1945.

Blaming, Chatto & Windus, 1976.

The Blush and Other Stories, Peter Davies, 1958.

A Dedicated Man, Peter Davies, 1965.

The Devastating Boys and Other Stories, Chatto & Windus, 1972.

A Game of Hide-and-Seek, Peter Davies, 1951.

Hester Lilly and Other Stories, Peter Davies, 1954.

In a Summer Season, Peter Davies, 1961.

Mrs Palfrey at the Claremont, Chatto & Windus, 1971.

Palladian, Peter Davies, 1946.

The Sleeping Beauty, Peter Davies, 1953.

The Soul of Kindness, Chatto & Windus, 1964.

A View of the Harbour, Peter Davies, 1947.

The Wedding Group, Chatto & Windus, 1968.

A Wreath of Roses, Peter Davies, 1949.

IVY COMPTON-BURNETT

Brothers and Sisters, Heath Cranton, 1925.

Darkness and Day, Gollancz, 1951.

Daughters and Sons, Gollancz, 1937.

Dolores, Edinburgh and London: Blackwood, 1911.

Elders and Betters, Gollancz, 1941.

A Family and a Fortune, Gollancz, 1939.

A Father and His Fate, Gollancz, 1957.

A God and His Gifts, Gollancz, 1963.

A Heritage and Its History, Gollancz, 1959.

A House and Its Head, Heinemann, 1935.

The Last and the First, Gollancz, 1971 (published posthumously).

Manservant and Maidservant, Gollancz, 1947 (New York: Alfred A. Knopf, 1949, under the title *Bullivant and the Lambs*).

Men and Wives, Heinemann, 1931.

The Mighty and Their Fall, Gollancz, 1961.

More Women than Men, Heinemann, 1933.

Mother and Son, Gollancz, 1955.

Parents and Children, Gollancz, 1941.

Pastors and Masters, Heath Cranton, 1925.

The Present and the Past, Gollancz, 1953.

Two Worlds and Their Ways, Gollancz, 1949.

ROBERT LIDDELL

FICTION

The Almond Tree, Jonathan Cape, 1954.

An Object for a Walk, Longmans, 1966.

The Deep End, Longmans, 1968.

The Gantillons, Jonathan Cape, 1940.

Kind Relations, Jonathan Cape, 1939.

The Last Enchantments, Jonathan Cape, 1948.

The Rivers of Babylon, Jonathan Cape, 1959.

Stepsons, Longmans, 1959.

Unreal City, Jonathan Cape, 1952.

Watering-Place, Jonathan Cape, 1945.

NON-FICTION

Aegean Greece, Jonathan Cape, 1954.

Byzantium and Istanbul, Jonathan Cape, 1956.

Cavafy: A Critical Biography, Duckworth, 1974.

Mainland Greece, Longmans, 1965.
The Morea, Jonathan Cape, 1958.
The Novels of George Eliot, Duckworth, 1977.
The Novels of Ivy Compton-Burnett, Gollancz, 1955.
The Novels of Jane Austen, Longmans, 1963.
Some Principles of Fiction, Jonathan Cape, 1953.
A Treatise on the Novel, Jonathan Cape, 1947.